BUSTER JOHNSTONE

FIRST CONTACT 02-2022

FIRST CONTACT 02-2022

iUniverse books may be ordered through booksellers or by contacting:

iUniverse
1663 Liberty Drive
Bloomington, IN 47403
www.iuniverse.com
844-349-9409

ISBN: 978-1-6632-2170-4 (sc)
ISBN: 978-1-6632-2171-1 (e)

Library of Congress Control Number: 2021908523

Print information available on the last page.

iUniverse rev. date: 05/28/2021

I was born on Cape Cod Massachusetts, April 18, 1960, I was born on Otis Air Forc where my dad was stationed. It is where I grew up my 5 or 6 years with my brother an sisters. It was pretty cool living there and when I grew older, started school, my mom wou have to dress us all in our snowsuits. As she would get to the end of dressing the rest of the kids, I would have my snowsuit off because it was too hot. She would have to put it back on me and then we would all walk to school. From what I remember it was a pretty long walk but it was good, because I loved playing in the snow. We had a big rock in our backyard, probably 20 feet tall. We would be able to play "King of The rock" in the winter time with 6-8 feet of snow around it and the first one to the top could push the other kids off. They would land in the snow so no one ever got hurt.

I always thought I was a little different than the rest of the kids. I'm not sure why, but they would say things; not that they were mean kids or anything, but it was something that I would have never even thought of. I would think different thoughts of more positive things and of a better way to confront the situation or subject of what was being talked about. So yes, I always thought I was kind of special and was not like the other kids. Not sure why, but something felt different about me.

My mom told me this story once, that I was in a little bassinet and they'd gone to the back of the station wagon and put groceries and stuff in the car to get ready to leave. When they left, they forgot me in the bassinet behind the car and back over me, but came out of it just fine. This was the first of many accidents to follow that I believe I've been watched over.

When I was 5 or 6 years old, we moved to Minnesota when my dad was going to Japan for a year. We rented a house in Waite Park Minnesota where we had family close by. That's what my dad wanted for my mom and all us kids while he was away. While we were living in that house, I had a little tree fort, probably fifteen - twenty feet up in this tree in my front yard. While I was up there one day, I slipped off the limb and fell backwards landing on my back. My head was two inches from hitting the concrete: . still hitting so hard that when my head bounced, my eyeball also bounced in their socket .at I had two gigantic black and blue eyes. My mom took me to the Military doctor and some time in the hospital with a concussion, but they got me fixed up. I think this was my Pineal Gland was activated.

Another tim .ne kitchen and a coffee pot cord ran from the counter down to the floor and chased iving in the same house, I was running around, chasing my little dog.. I .ne counter which plugged into the coffee pot. Running after my dog, hooked the bac anked it down, spilling the fresh made coffee on my foot.. It was so hot that when I took my sock off, it peeled all the skin off my foot also.. So off to the doctor i go again they bandage my foot, fixing me right up. However, this time, they take me into a separate room with a police officer and the doctor asks my mother to leave the room. By now, this is the second major incident within two months and now they're asking me questions. Questions like what happened and if my mother was abusing me or if I was just that clumsy and unlucky. I told him exactly what happened and then they let us go home.

A year went by and we moved back to Massachusetts wehn my dad came back from his duty in Japan. We weren't there long before he got stationed in Mississippi. And Mississippi was quite a culture shock. I grew up on a Military Base for most of my life before this move and had many friends of different races and color. But when I got to Mississippi, we would be walking downtown and I would see drinking fountains for the white people and drinking fountains for the black people. I was quite confused, especially when we got on the school bus and the black people had to go to the back of the bus while I had to sit in front. It even came to blows at the apartment complex we lived at where my mom had totten into a fight with a black woman for some reason I can't remember. That's when my mom and dad had to sit me down to explain to me about how people look down on other races of people. So I had a hard time thinking 'wow, what the rest of the world was like if it was like this here.' But I came back to the point of being different and thinking differently than most people. I seem to get along with everyone so after our stay in Mississippi, my dad received orders to go to Florida while the rest of his Squadron received orders to go to California. Just at the last moment, for some reason, his orders were changed to also go to California. Now there are several families heading west, so my mom gathered me, my brother and my sisters because we were riding with Mrs. Stewart in her station wagon with her six boys to California. After arriving, we moved in and lived on base housing in North Highlands while our house was being built in Orangevale.

My story started in 1969 when my dad was transferred from Otis Air Force Base in Cape Cod Massachusetts to McClellan Air Force Base in North Highlands California. We lived on base housing and I went to Larchmont Elementary School. Miss Rhody, my fourth grade teacher and a good one too. She taught us strange things about the Zodiac Signs and about the Bermuda Triangle. I was pretty much hooked. I would talk about Aliens and wonder about them; that was pretty much my topic of conversation.

I was nine when we moved here waiting for our house to be built in Orangevale and we would come watch that every other weekend or so. I spent probably the first year in North Highlands and then we finally moved into our new house on Greenacres Way in 1970. I was in the garage with my dad from the age of nine until I was 18. My brother could go play, one of my sister's could go play and my other sister could go play, but I had to be in the garage with my dad and not by choice. If I didn't have homework or baseball practice or games, I was in the garage. My dad welded, he worked on cars, refrigeration and took college courses up to the day he died in 1982; he was 49 years old.

I did a lot of talking while we worked on whatever project was going on at that time. About Aliens and the Bermuda Triangle, the Blue Hole and the Zodiac Signs. I started hearing about Aliens; tried to put them all together but didn't really know if they all had to do something with each other, but I wondered a lot. Whether we were cleaning engines or refrigerators, taking things apart, fixing them and learning a lot; I would talk about Aliens and the other subject all the time and her really never said anything and I wasn't sure why, but I would always talk. My dad and I were in the car one time going to an auction out at McClellan and bid on boxes that you could not look in and if you won the bid, you won the box. It would be like Christmas looking in those boxes because you never knew what you would get. Sometimes it would be tools, sometimes it would be electrical connectors and just a variety of things. I really liked going to the auctions! My brother would even come sometimes. One time we won a bid on a box of kites. I still have mine, but need to get a new cover for it. So coming back from the auctions with my dad one time, I was, you guessed it, talking about Aliens; I don't remember how old I was exactly, but between fifteen and seventeen. By now, my dad was a little frustrated, pulled the car over to the side of the road, turned the engine off, looked me straight in the eyes and said I am so tired of hearing about Aliens.

He said "I'm going to tell you two things and after that, I don't ever want to hear about Aliens again". He said that he was classified in his job description and most of the stuff he worked on was top secret. One of the things he told me was that when he used to leave, he would get a call, have to grab his bag and leave. We never knew where he went and we never knew what he did. He told me in confidence that his main job was to operate the A-Wax Rotating Radar in the Constellation; an airplane commonly known as "The Connie" while flying above Air Force One. This was his job anytime The U.S. President had to fly anywhere. My dad was the Radar Technician that could track anything around The President's plane for a hundred miles while flying 20 miles above Air Force One protecting it. He went on to say, one of his jobs involved flying through the Bermuda Triangle. I could just imagine what he saw on the radar screen, but he pretty much just left it at that. He didn't go on about that subject anymore and only left me to wonder.

He finally went on to tell me about an abandoned Air Force Base they went to. There they went in a two hundred by four hundred airplane hanger; definitely for very large planes. When they entered, they saw a perfectly round burn spot centered from one side of the hanger floor to the other. Against both sides of the 400 foot long walls, there were 1 ½ foot wide by 4 foot tall dust images side by side the length of each wall. Images of cubicles and each one had two refrigerators ports coming from them keeping something very cold. You can guess, my imagination went crazy for what 200 to 300 Alien Beings they had frozen in there. But after he was done telling me that, never going into details, said he told this to me to get the point across; Aliens are real. He also said he never wanted to hear me talkin about Aliens again.

That's when I got my confirmation from him.

My dad served in the Air Force until he retired in 1970 and we never spoke about anything he did ever again. He passed away in 1982. At his life celebration after his funeral service, some of the air force buddies he served with were there; These were also the families we traveled from Massechusettes to California together all those years earlier. I thought I'd talk to them about what my dad told me years earlier. I walked to Mr. Stewart, and said "hey Jim, my dad told me about these two things and I was just wondering what you think about it?" He looked at me while putting his arm around my shoulder and said "come on Buster, lets go have a beer". It was apparent he wasn't going to tell me anything.

I continued looking around and then saw Mr. Taylor, deciding to walk over to see if he would answer my question. After asking Frank the same question, he only says, "come on Buster, lets go get something to eat". They never said yes, but it definitely was not a no, even if apparent he too was not going to tell me anything.

Now Mr. Smith, he's the one I really wanted to talk to, so walked over where he was standing very near my dad's open casket. "Smitty", I stated and went on to tell him those two things my dad told me all those years earlier. I didn't realize he would get so angry about it, but he did and started grinding on me about how "your dad was Top Secret, he should have never said any of those things he told you!!" He went on saying "we were Classified" and he DID NOT EVER want to hear me repeat any of what my dad told me and to forget he ever told me. The way all three of his buddies reacted and changed the subject immediately, even getting angry was further confirmation that what my dad had shared was so very true. From then on, I didn't only think Aliens were real, I knew they were real.

I lived in a house at Rich Hill Drive in Orangevale CA by myself. During this time alone, my car quit working and I needed to borrow my mom's car. She lived three blocks away so after work each night, I would drop her car off and walk home. This is when I noticed the orange, almost like a light kind of hidden behind the fences,behind the bushes and behind the trees which followed me home. This went on for several weeks until I got my car fixed, but it never showed itself to me - at that time.

Later there was this girl who needed a place to stay, so helping her out, let her move her things in the back bedroom of my three bedroom home. Not long after she moved in, I noticed my cat started to scratch; she never scratched. Concerned about my cat scratching, I went into the bedroom and in all the girl's stuff could see all the tiny fleas jumping around everywhere. Thousands of them, everywhere. Had to do something about that, so I went up to the local hardware store and bought a few flea bombs. I put two in her bedroom, one each in the other two bedrooms, one in the kitchen and one in the living room. It was late, but I couldn't stay home, so put my cat outside, grabbed my telescope, jumped in my truck and headed up eastbound Highway 50. I didn;t have any particular destination in mind, other than wanting to be totally outside the light pollution. I'm not sure of the exit I took, but ended up going down this frontage road eventually seeing this dirt road off to the right. In the dark through the trees, I meandered down the road and eventually it came to a large clearing, rectangular in size. My guess is it had to be at least two hundred feet long and one hundred feet wide. There was a large unlit warehouse type building at one end, so I pulled up closer to that. Really liking the unlit area I found, got out of my truck, set my telescope up and started looking around just to see what peaked my interest. This clearing I was in, you could see treetops from where I was all the way down to the other end.

As I was standing by my telescope, suddenly this Orange Ord came flying very fast up over the trees, then down to head height and came right up towards me. It was probably three feet away from me and slowed down like something you would see in a cartoon. It was moving fast, but like seeing it in sections.

It went about two or three feet past my right side and stopped and then took the same exact path it came from, going back up over the trees, then it was gone. I mean it was fast! The whole experience may have been only about eight seconds and I wasn't sure what that was all about, but figured it was a warning and I wasn't taking any chances. I felt like it was the same Orange Orb that would follow me when walking home at night after returning my mom's car. I ended up taking a drive on the way home because I knew I had to be gone long enough for the flea bombs to dissipate, hopefully killing all the fleas.

Some time had passed and I was sure it was safe to go home, got there and the flea bombs worked. All the fees were dead, but now everything in the house had to be cleaned and wiped down, but wasn't done watching the stars, looking at the Constellations or looking for satellites flying back and forth across the sky. One day I saw a small airplane and then noticed it did not have any blinking lights, like ALL our flying crafts have.

I grabbed my binoculars and as I was watching this little airplane not flying too far away, I saw this Orange Orb come flying up to it. It was basketball in size, just like the one I saw up in the mountains in that clearing I came to when meandering down that dirt road. It started to appear as if playing with the plane, moving quickly to the front or it, straight to the back, then over to one wing tip and then the other. I thought it was weird, but also thought it was the same Orange Orb I saw walking home from my mom;'s house and in the mountains.

One day while watching TV, I saw a Preview for a Documentary show about Foo Fighter. After the commercials ended and the Documentary came back on, the Narrator started talking about these basketball size Orange Orbs called Foo Fighters. The Narrator went on to say, they were eventually named by the military pilots from different nations because these Orbs would fly all around their planes,even seeming to chase them. These were pilots from the old military airplanes in the 1940s, '50s and '60s and their stories being told of this orange orb these pilots of these military planes we're seeing right outside their window. These things flew beside them in front of them and never touched their airplanes just kind of played with them. For a while, the French thought it was the Germans, the Germans thought it was the Americans and the Americans thought it was the Russians. After that program,I knew these Orbs have been around for a long time. There seemed to be this one certain Orb that was alway around me. I called it Spot. There were other times, I would see a White Orb and I called it Dot. I was out in my backyard again and again just looking up in the night sky.

I was in my backyard late one evening looking up toward the fence over the retaining wall above me watching the sky when I noticed this Orange Orb came flying past the trees in the next yard over my fence and right past me again. It was again about three feet away and it looked the same way it did when I took the telescope up to the clearing I found in the mountains. Once again, it zoomed back over the fence and up over the trees the same way it came.

I had wondered if anybody else had seen this orange orb so I talked to my cousin about it. He ran a concrete company that I worked for as a laborer for twenty-two years. He told me that he went camping once and he and several of the campers in his group we're out for a walk when they saw the orange orb and could not believe it themselves.

I had gone out to Mather air Force Base a few times and saw some strange lights out there and asked my cousin Todd if he wanted to go one night; he said sure so it was dark when we went out there and parked by the side of the road. There was a little shack on the inside of this fenced off property. I told him I saw this weird light out there one time and we should look for something. I told him to go one way and I went the other way and all of a sudden there was this light that was on top of the pole over the shack and it looked just like a regular light on a pole. But then this light started drifting towards us and I asked Todd if he was seeing the same thing. He said he sure did. It started drifting around and then it drifted over towards this other Pole and it went behind the pole and disappeared. Todd looked at me and said now that's pretty strange Bub. I replied with yes it is Todd and then told him to go that way and I'd go this way and see if we can see around the back side of the pole. Just then I barely see the light, almost like it was peeking out from behind the pole and then dipped back behind the pole. I told Todd that light is playing peek-a-boo with us and it did it again and again and then it started drifting back towards the building where it stayed by the pole that it started from. I told him to go down the fence line one way and I went down the other way and as I was looking down the fence line I was seeing off in the distance another light. I called him to come over and look and between these other two buildings, we saw this light moving around these buildings. It went up the top of the building and then down and around the building. Nobody's that tall to have a flashlight and able to shine that high so we didn't know what it was. By then it was getting late and someone driving a car inside the fence started driving over to us. It was pretty far away at the time but we decided it was time to go. He did finally see something very strange with me and said "I got to give it to you Bub, that was quite interesting". See, I would tell him about these things I would see and he thought I was nuts until I told him about the orange orb which turn out he also said he saw. And now that he saw this other light at Mather air Force Base he could not call me crazy anymore.

Another time I had to go pick up my mom from UC Davis on Stockton Boulevard and I showed up probably twenty to thirty minutes before she was able to leave. When I arrived to her room the doctor was just leaving telling her she could get dressed and go home, she grabbed her clothes and went into the bathroom. I was standing in her room looking out the window which was facing south as I could see a mountain range way out there which had to have been a hundred miles away. As I was looking at this mountain range I started to see these lines come out of the mountain, rose up and go forward when another one followed right behind it drifting up and went forward. There were probably ten of these things that left this mountain too. From where I was, I could see that they looked to be a half inch long, but if they were a hundred miles away and looked a half an inch long, whoa how long were they if you were up close to them. My mom came out of the bathroom and I remembered she didn't really want to talk about anything to do on this subject. I didn't even talk to her about it. We just went downstairs to the car and I took her home. To this day that was one of the craziest things I ever saw because if my distance perception was correct, they had to have been a couple miles long if they were a hundred miles away . I really didn't have anybody to talk to and my mom didn't want to hear it. People that I told stories to would listen but then they'd never come back or want to hear any more stories. Nobody ever asked me anymore than a little bit and I had nobody to talk to for many years about any of this. I had all this kept inside me as I was being shown all these things that I'm sure not too many people had ever seen before.

Another night I was sitting in the house because it was raining, but later the weather cleared up and I went outside to look up. I heard this whirring noise which was very strange, like something was spinning real fast in the sky, but I couldn't see anything.

The sky was still partially cloudy and as I was watching them, Still hearing the whirring noise, I noticed they were not blowing in one direction or another due to the weather. Instead it was this seemingly mile wide clumps of clouds all over the sky, all spinning in one direction, forming smaller cut-out images. I kept watching and then realized all these different clumps of clouds were spinning in a circular direction throughout the sky. But the weird thing was each clump of cloud was being cut into a shape of the Zodiac Signs. I saw Sagittarius, Pisces and other Signs being formed from each one of these clouds as the whole group of them spun in one direction like a whole part of something.

Learning about the Zodiac Signs in Miss Rohde's fourth grade class and the Plaque my mom and dad owned in their import store.

My mom and dad owned a Mexican Import Store where they also sold Permanent Press Fatigues which had just come out on the market. Their store was the only store in California to sell these. Each weekend, one of us kids would get to go with my mom to the store. We'd play the pinball machine and go searching around the property looking for other stuff. We got to go to lunch wherever we wanted to go, so going to the store with mom was a fun day. Well in this store was this Zodiac Sign Plaque which my mom gave me that Christmas. So growing up with the knowledge of the Zodiac Signs, I know a lot about what they look like to say that's what I saw in the sky that night.

The following morning I got up and did my usual things, had breakfast, took a shower, sat there and watched some TV and while sitting there, started to hear this whirring noise outside again. Now the storm was over and it had not rained since early the day before; so I went outside for a look up to see a few clouds in the sky over my house, spinning in a circle and began taking shape, just like the massive cloud from the day before being formed into the Zodiac Signs. I never saw what was causing the whirring noise, or what was creating these shapes to be so vivid. It was very weird, but also really cool.

After that, there were days I would go out and just look around staring up at the sky looking for things, I decided I would go get my binoculars and just started looking around then laid down on my concrete patio and as I was looking up straight up I saw a little tiny white ball way, way up there. I mean it was way up there and every day I went out, I would grab my binoculars around the same time of day, sometimes later and sometimes maybe sooner. I'd lay down on the pad and look up and that same thing would be in the same spot all day, no matter what. Anytime of the day I looked up with those binoculars that thing was always, always there. It didn't matter what time in the afternoon, so I knew it wasn't a star. I was starting to see more and more things that seemed like they were just for me to see. Like the times I would take my son home, having him all weekend and that was great being with my son during those times I took him home. When I was leaving to go back home I kind of got turned around or was led down some other streets, trying to find my way out. I turned down this one Street and as I was driving down, it came to an end with a white barrier, so you couldn't drive any further. I saw a field and turned my truck lights off and just decided to get out there and was looking across the field and these little lights started flashing. I mean all over this gigantic field little tiny lights not emitting light but just flashing. And to go along with that, one night I was out searching the skies and as I was looking around one part of the sky and only one part of the sky, I saw a massive amount of lights flashing; there had to be hundreds of these little flashing lights just in one part of the sky.

It was very strange; I couldn't understand it and didn't know how to explain. Then one day I was watching TV and a Jeep commercial came on and in the background of this commercial behind these Jeeps I could see it was kind of turning night but not dark. I saw the same thing; they had these little flashing lights up in the sky, just in one part of the sky, just like I saw. I'm pretty sure somebody who was putting that commercial together had seen the same thing I saw that one night just a while back because it wasn't too much longer after that I saw the commercial.

My friends and I were walking through a shopping center one time and we walked into Pier 1 imports and I started staring at this poster which was rather strange because it had the same image line after line after line after line printed from the top down to the bottom. I thought that was kind of strange because it wasn't normal. One of my friends said that you're supposed to be able to look into the picture and see like a cutout of another picture. So I stared into it and started to try to bend my mind which he said you were supposed to do to be able to get the image to come out. I wasn't sure what that meant but I looked into it. None of the friends I was with had been able to see it, but while I was trying to do this, I started to see three horses running. So I told my friends that's what I saw and they looked on the back of the poster and that's exactly what was printed on the back as to what you were supposed to see in the image. I looked into other pictures that were on the wall and I saw two dolphins jumping in one of them. I saw other pictures looking into the other images. One of the friends I was with asked me to come up to his mom and dad's house up in shingle springs. His name was Mark Katzen and his dad was

Alan and his mom was Jan. But they were gone for the weekend and we were sitting, watching TV and he pulled out this book that was under the coffee table in the cabinet, opened it and it was a book of the same thing I saw at Pier 1 imports of the posters. and I started looking into these pictures that were in the book and I immediately was able to pick out what was hidden in each one of these prints. I turned the page and I would almost automatically be able to see each image hidden in the picture. Now my friends were still not able to see these things. I would see these posters in different places, different stores and it was pretty cool to be able to look at them and pretty much automatically see what was hidden in them. I knew that I could stand further away, and even further away and would still be able to see them by trying to pull the image in the middle, closer to my mind. And the further away I got, the more I had to try to pull it into my mind. Well by doing this, I was slightly crossing my eyes and the further away I went, I had to cross my eyes a little more. I smoked pot at that time and it would be easier to be able to see these images after doing so.

I have seen many shows with these energy swirls like a maze; it starts out at one point and then winds into the middle. I've seen them in cave art on stones in books. I mean many programs have talked about them in the Ancient Alien shows and a lot of the ancient warfare shows have seen them also.

I was sitting in my living room one day, the sun was out, but the day was almost over and the sun was coming down in my backyard. A ray of light came through the back window and as I was staring out the window sitting on my couch the ray of light reflected off of something around me and hit the ceiling above the sliding glass door that I was looking out, so i started to stare at this light. I had taken a puff of weed and was just kind of sitting there staring at this blob of light that had reflected up on the ceiling. While staring at the light I started to try to pull it in closer to me and as I pulled it closer in my mind, a rectangle formed. I sat and stared at the rectangle and saw that the rectangle had gray scales all across it uniformly. Now I sat and stared at this rectangle trying to pull it closer and all of the sudden an eyelid opened up and a black eye was staring right at me. Whoa, so I stared back at this eyeball and wasn't really thinking about anything; just wow - look at this! I stared it down; it was probably 15-20 seconds as I was looking at it. It was like the face that the eyeball was in and it did not close its eye. Instead it turned its head and when it turned it was like the nose would be a divider and then I turned, going past the divider and the whole image became the scaly rectangle again. Now I never saw a whole face or head, it was just the eyeball and the way the head turned when the eyeball disappeared, it was a right eyeball so I know this being had two eyes and it was just showing me the right eye. I imagine that somebody in the way past had seen this before and this is what became the all seeing eye that is on the dollar bill on top of the pyramid and in Egyptian writings, Hieroglyphics and signs from the Freemasons and other Ancient Tribes that I've seen on the show, Ancient Aliens. It's a common sight and somebody in the past saw the same thing I did. Shows that I have seen have described and explained that we have a Pineal Gland in our brain. It is a rice sized gland in the middle of our brain and needs to be activated. I believe my Pineal Gland was activated when I fell out of a tree in Minnesota in Waite Park. So I started practicing mind-bending and as I practiced, I would ask people to come out to the backyard and it was only at night. I would ask them to watch me because I felt myself vibrating and I knew something was happening. While they were watching me I asked them just to see what they saw and let me know what they saw as I was doing this. After I was done I'd ask what did you see? The response I got was that I disappeared from my head down to my toes and that they could see through me. It was just black some said and they saw what looked like stars through me, like little white specks.

So I practiced some more and got to the point where I asked a couple neighbors Kent and Jan to come by. They came over one night and I asked them to stand where I was asking everybody else to stand and I stood probably 25-30 feet away from them and proceeded to do this. After I was done I looked at them and asked well what did you see? Jan spoke up and said, what do you think we saw so I said I believe you saw me disappear. She jumped up out of her seat and said, now if you're doing that you better stop because that's not natural and I don't believe that you should be doing that. She said it like she was upset. I just kind of looked at her and said okay well thank you so I'm pretty sure they saw me disappear. Then probably a week or two later, I saw Terry and Brad who were other neighbors, out walking around the neighborhood. I had seen them walking around the neighborhood even late at night when I got home late. I asked them if they would come over the following night. And wow, the response I got from them was "we will never come over to your house at night, there is no way we will enter your house at night. We will come over in the daytime, that's no problem but never at night. Well I took that as late at night when I was practicing in my house doing this mind bending that I'm pretty sure they saw on their walk late at night that my house disappeared. I was pretty sure by the tone that I got from them and as serious as they were when they told me that they would not come over to my house at night. During this time, I showed my son what I did. I also showed my sister Jean, and my future wife Judy. I also showed some of my friends and they said the same thing.

I got really curious as to what the mind-bending was all about and if there was some literature on it. I looked for some books by myself but I couldn't find any and went to the library which had just got computers installed there. I did not know how to use the computer so I asked the librarian how to look up a book, she set the computer up and said now all I have to do is type in the subject of the kind of book I was looking for. I typed in changing the frequency of your body by using your mind. I waited for the computer to do its thing and what popped up was one book. I can't remember the name of the book but there was only one book so I checked to see if I could check it out, and it said that it was unavailable. So I found out there was a book on the subject but only one and you can't look at it. Somebody doesn't want you finding out anymore about that subject.

Someone in the past could either do what I was able to do or they saw someone do what I was able to do and wrote a book about it. I pretty much had to just let it go with finding a book or something about it and just figured what the heck would I have learned by reading that book. Did it have something to do with being able to levitate objects or levitate myself. I do have dreams and have had dreams in the past of myself levitating.

For some reason I got a call from a friend. She was moving and she was selling some stuff and asked if I wanted to come over to see what she had to sell and if I wanted anything. I went over to check what she had and saw a box that said Polaroid Camera which was new and still in the box. So I think I gave her $20 for it and stopped at Raley's at the4 corner of Madison and Hazel Avenues and bought a couple packs of film. I got home and put a pack of film in it and started taking some pictures to see if it worked and how it worked. My family had a Polaroid Camera many years before this and it was made by Kodak but Kodak had taken the idea from Polaroid and got sued. There was a big court case and Kodak lost so we had to return our Kodak Polaroid Camera and get our money back. I took some pictures as it started getting dark. I had gone outside and was just looking around and then saw what looked like a star. It was way up in the sky but the stars were moving and it didn't; it just sat there. It was getting darker, so I took a picture of it and a little while later, I took another picture of it. The darker it got, I kept taking pictures of it. Now as I took the pictures, I'd set them in the house to finish developing but first I had put them in my pocket for a few seconds to take a few more pictures. I went in the house and took the pictures out of my pocket and set them on the back of my recliner chair to finish developing. I went back outside, took some more pictures and brought them in to let them finish developing on the back of my chair. I picked up the ones that were already developed and started to stack them and went outside and started taking another picture or two or three of the same thing up in the sky. I brought them in to set them on the back of the chair, when I picked up the other pictures that were developed two of the pictures had a strange image on them. I looked at them later after taking some more pictures. The two pictures with the images on them looked as though it was a fingerprint so I thought it was my finger, that I touched the pictures too long when I put them in my pocket and then when I took them out to set them on the back of the chair. Figured my finger stayed on the picture too long while it was developing, and had somehow transferred my fingerprint onto the pictures.

I took pictures of my cat Mesha because through the years that I had her, twenty or twenty-one years, she had an image of what we know as The Grey Alien. I looked at the pictures to see if the image came out correctly and sure enough I could see the image of an Alien on her back. I put the pictures in my drawer and didn't think much more about them for a while.

It was probably four or five years they were in the drawer when I was watching TV and this commercial came on about Polaroid Cameras. The actors were of these guys in the park and one was taking the pictures. As it came out of the camera and while developing, he flung it to another friend, like a frisbee. Then that guy flung it at another guy which they were probably twenty to thirty feet away from each other. As they caught them, they were touching them while they were still developing. So I knew I didn't touch my picture any longer than any of those guys did, I went and grabbed my pictures out of my drawer to look at them again . I knew then that that couldn't be my fingerprint and when I looked at the pictures again,

FIRST CONTACT

Okay so when I took the pictures out of my drawer and took another look at them the fingerprint on one of the pictures, I could tell, was definitely not mine. The print image went up the finger from bottom to top, to the point of the finger where the point hadn't even touched the film. You could see where the finger actually touched the film. And then what I'm saying is the radiation in their system was able to catch the role of the tip of the finger.

So the fingerprint actually went from bottom to top and went up like a fountain, like water in a fountain was squirting straight up the middle of the finger and the lines came out from the center of the finger like it would in a water fountain, I knew right then what this was; I knew it was an Alien's fingerprint.

Now the other Polaroid picture that had the other image in it looked as if you could line it up with the first one and when you put the two pictures together you could tell that at the top of the two pictures in the center they were pinched together by this Being. When held together, a seven inch long finger came to light there. It was in perfect detail, you could even see the webbing of the hand at the very end of the picture all the way up to where the finger touched both Prints. And it formed what definitely looked like a finger that was seven inches long. I took my magnifying glass out and wow, the detail you could see in the prints themselves. The colors were vibrant, not smudged, not smeared and absolutely perfect definition.

When I looked at the seven inch long finger, I saw what looked to be knuckles in the center of the finger and the image of where the knuckles would have been. The round spot was burnt and cracked in both spots. So what I'm saying is the radiation from them flying around in space has collected in their body and bones and joints. Most likely the joints contain most of the radiation and when the Alien Being touched the photographs while they were developing, the radiation from the knuckles burnt and cracked the image of where the knuckles would have been. Like

I said, I knew what these were after I took them out of my drawer five years, which was a long time span until I saw that commercial.

They gave me these pictures for some reason. They led me to that girl's house and bought that camera and picked up those two packs of film, It was all for the reason of me getting these prints to bring out at some point to prove that Aliens are real.

So once I did this and figured it all out, I called my sister Jean. I knew she had a computer and I didn't know much about them. I figured if I took my pictures over there, she could somehow put them on the computer so other people could see them and comment on them and hopefully get some kind of talk going out in public. So other people that were interested could see them and maybe, I could talk to them and tell them some of my story.

My sister Jean did put them on the Internet; she had this scanner thing which she scanned them into to put them on the computer screen. I saw them go in and then saw them on the screen. I appreciated her doing and told her thank you and that I would call her to find out from time to time if anyone had commented.

I didn't wait long, probably a week and called her to ask if anyone had made any comment or response of any kind but she said no, not yet. I let it go another two or three weeks and called her again to ask, and once again she said no, she didn't see any comments or anybody responding to the pictures. Again I waited another week or two thinking, wow this is long enough, I was sure someone would have commented by then because these were pretty interesting.

When I called her two or three weeks after that she still said no. Well this was going on for two months,.so I called her and told her I was coming over just to take a look at the pictures and see myself. I got over there, went in and asked her to pull the pictures up on the screen so I could see and make sure everything was good; and if I could see any comments or some kind of response. She pulled the pictures up to where the picture should be but when she tried to get them up on the screen, they were gone. The pictures had somehow been taken down or off or whatever happens.

Now like I said I don't know much about computers, very little, but I know that once you put something out there, it's somewhere, it's there somewhere. Well she couldn't find it anywhere they were just gone. She had saved them somehow on the computer and even went to where she saved them, the pictures were gone. So I said okay I guess it's not time to have the pictures out there, I knew there was a reason they were taken off.

I figured it wasn't time for them to be out there so I put them in my drawer and kept them safe for the next twenty years. always asking when I should pull these out. I know there's going to be a time. I know you will let me know when it is time to bring these pictures out and show the world.

I would bring them out and show friends from time to time. Those who were interested in the subject but kept them close by. They never went anywhere away from me any further than the twenty to thirty feet back in my bedroom where I kept them.. I kept him safe and in my room for the twenty years after I did the computer thing at my sister's when they were taken off the computer.

I kept asking when is this supposed to happen, when am I supposed to bring these out to show the world? And for the next twenty years it was pretty silent. For those twenty years and was also when I was learning the most about them. They were showing me the most about themselves and then comes 2016 and I'm watching TV, the Ancient Alien Show, to be exact and I see that there is going to be the first alien convention ever in Santa Clara Southern California. So I got on the phone and figured out how to get my ticket, found a motel close and made my arrangements for a registration of three days and two nights at the motel. The alien convention was Thursday,Friday and Saturday. It was at the end of October I remember. because there was a costume party for Halloween on Saturday night.

Then I started thinking, oh my gosh! Should I even be bringing these pictures out now? I have no idea if this is the right time to do this so I asked, in my mind, please show me something like you have shown me before. All of these things like the Orange Orbs, the twinkling lights, the All Seeing Eye; please show me something that I am supposed to be bringing these pictures to this Alien Convention and bringing them out to the world. That's how I would get my answers by clues and then putting the clues together as to the answer to my question. It was four, five or six months before the convention was going to be so I waited for my clue.

My wife and I had planned a trip up to Silver Lake. It's up on highway 88 at the top of the mountains, elevation is 7500 or 8000 feet. We went camping and it was great; had a real good time. But on the third day we got up in the morning and we're making our plans for the day; and I always look up,. so as I was looking around I could see that there was this light up in the sky, it was way light enough to not be a star and you couldn't see anything else in the sky except this light and was sitting there, pretty far up. As I was looking at it, I kind of walked over to three trees and made a triangle out of the image in the sky of the light and marked a spot on the ground where I could stand there later on, because it didn't look like it was moving.

We had made our plans for the day and went out and we'd probably gone for four or five hours traveling around looking for trails that we would walk and see different sites and we even stopped at another campground way up the road to check it out for a later time it was a great day. We decided to head back and when we got back to our campsite, we started getting ready to make some dinner. Well I had kind of forgotten about the light but as soon as I looked up in the sky and saw that it was still there, I walked over to where I marked the ground and found a triangle between the three trees and that light was in the same exact spot as when we left five hours ago. It looked like the same light and the same distance away as the one I took the polaroid pictures of that night some twenty-plus years ago. That night my wife started getting tired and for some reason I wasn't really tired so I sat up. She went to bed but we couldn't get her CPAP Machine to run all night on the battery we got charged and she ended up going into the truck and laying down on the seat spending the rest of the night.

So I had the tent by myself and I would just lay there; I couldn't sleep for nothing! I was so wide awake, it was unreal because I've never been that wide awake that late at night! It had to be three or four o'clock in the morning. It was so late and I'm just laying there wishing I could sleep. As I was laying there

I started to hear just a staticy, electrical type noise which wasn't real loud, but it was very intense! I stepped out of the tent and walked around where I could hear the noise and then the noise had stopped. Where I thought it had stopped, I looked through the trees where I saw the top of the granite mountain.You could see it was probably a mile and a half away and it had a flat top, You could also probably see about a mile of the flat top until a bunch of trees got in the way. Even with all the trees I could look through them and could see the top of the flat mountain perfectly, I sat there looking at an orange and reddish light that filled the top of that mile-long flat ridge on top of that mountain; it just creeped right up to the edge and sat there. Now the noise had stopped whirling but I could still hear it so I knew that it was the noise I was looking at and this image I'm seeing was of this orange and reddish bar of light. That thing up on the top of the mountain was the spaceship I saw up in the sky as the light that I tracked and kept into view during the day was one in the same. I knew at that time that was my confirmation from them, and I knew that was my clue I was supposed to be taking these pictures out of my drawer after twenty years of waiting and wondering when to do it. The time was now I was supposed to be going to this Alien Convention and letting the world know that Alien Beings are real and that I am in contact with them is the reason why I have these pictures.

So for the next few months until the Alien Convention was scheduled to be, I would ask in my mind when should I be saying that first contact is going to be, and I waited for my clue and waited for my clue quite patiently too I might add because this was getting pretty exciting. Then about three months before the convention, I started being woken up every morning at 2:22am every morning. I mean every morning at the same time. I would roll over and look at my clock and it was 2:22am and this went on for three months until the convention. What I deduce from this is that February 2nd 2022 is going to be the first contact. Now it could be that it's February 22nd of '22, but why just the three numbers that could only really be up there unless I had military time going on, which I didn't. That was February 2nd, the 2nd month of the year, the 2nd day of the year and the 22nd year which is 02/02/2022. So in that time I was waiting and got a hold of MUFON, the Mutual UFO Network and my investigator that I got in contact with was Valerie Benco. I told her what I had going on and that I needed to make an appointment with her to show her these pictures and tell her some of my story and that we are going to have first contact on February 2nd of 22 and how I got my pictures.

She made an appointment with me at the Denny's in Rocklin and I went to this appointment with her to give my story, to show her these pictures and even give her copies of what I had. When I got there and went inside, I looked around and could tell that this lady I saw looking across the room looking at me was Valerie and she had another lady with her who turned out to be Devlin Runge. She is the head investigator in our area, so I told them some of my story, kind of how things happened, how they came about, how I got the pictures and that we were going to have first contact in February 2022. I also gave them copies of my pictures. Now Valerie was to take all this information and make a report on it and create a file to put it in. I've made case investigations for MUFON. So when I looked later at the file which was number 81501, there wasn't much of what I said typed in and I couldn't find the pictures anywhere, but like I said I'm pretty computer illiterate so I couldn't find how to bring them up. But during the meeting, Valerie and Devlin and I Valerie were very-very-very excited, Devlin pretty much just blew me off and came up with all kinds of reasons and ideas why this couldn't be what I'm saying it is. It was pretty disheartening because I knew she had 'the say so' over Valerie and what Valerie could put in the report. There wasn't even anything about first contact being in 2022. So I didn't have much faith in the direction on the avenue I tried to take and I waited for the convention to come up.

So the time for the convention was coming up and I was getting very excited! I headed down to L.A., driving not flying. I could see the lights flashing up in the sky as I'm driving along. I know they're right there. I see them flash around me all the time. I know that they're in the next dimension and are following me and are with me all the time. They have saved my life way more than three times.

So as I'm driving along seeing them flash me up in the sky with white flashes and black flashes I get to my motel and get situated, go out and get something to eat. I got there in the early morning so after breakfast, I went to the convention and checked out the Friday activities where I saw the activities that were going to be that day and were some of the most interesting. I picked out one that the producers and a lot of the cast from Ancient Aliens we're going to be; like Giorgio tsoukalos, David childress, Linda Moulton Howe and even Billy mumy from Lost In Space who is a consultant for the show and their executive producer and some of the co-producers. I found my seat and was in a good spot. I was probably twenty rows from the front, kind of in the middle of the audience and as the show started, Ken Burns, Producer of the show started talking to the crowd; I kind of interrupted him when he was talking about the next segments of the show and what we could expect out of them. I kind of jumped up and said I have an Alien fingerprint and a seven inch long finger onto polaroid prints. He said wow that could be our next show as he looked at the co-producers of the show. He said they would like to see the pictures but if I could wait until after the talk and if I could bring them up and show them afterwards. I said sure and as I was about to sit down I started hearing, 'hey can I see those' from people in the crowd, so I left my seat and started to walk around and show people these two Polaroid's that if you put them together show a seven inch long finger and a fingerprint that is not of this world was imprinted on them and how the detail is so defined that these are what they are. I walked around and showed many, many people throughout the stadium. When the producer and all the guest stars we're done and everybody got their talk out of their system, I went up towards the front as the crowd started to disperse and stood up where the producers and guest stars were all getting ready to leave. I caught them on their way out and showed them the pictures and I told them that first contact was going to be February 2022. They said that they would like to compare them to some of the images they have already collected and when they were going to do a show on this subject they would contact me and get me to L.A. and would go over the pictures and my story. They took my phone number and name and thanked me and said they would get in touch with me. Well I waited and waited and waited. I tried to get a hold of MUFON to see if anybody was looking at my pictures and looking at my story and absolutely no one had.

At the alien convention I had shown many of the vendors and all of the cast of the Ancient Alien Show, except Erich Von Daniken, the godfather of ufology wasn't at this one, but most of the others were. I saw Nick Pope at another convention center. I showed as many people as I could. I walked around to all the vendors and showed the main people at their booths and some looked at my pictures, some wanted more of my story but all were wowed.

As I walked around I saw a booth that had a spiritual medium and her name was Skeeter. I spent the fourty dollars to have a session with her and it was very interesting. She read the Tarot Cards and told me that she had never seen the cards come up in any kind of fashion the way they came up for my reading.. She's then said she was going to try to contact the Being that was looking over me and that gave me the pictures. She held the pictures close to her because I took the originals there to show people and while she was holding the originals she fell into a trance and got in contact with the Being and she told me his name was Egzyt.. So I asked some questions and found this to be very interesting because the entity was answering my questions to the answers that I had already come up with being very close to the same.

I waited and waited for them to contact me and for MUFON to contact me to get this going. I had also talked to a regional head of MUFON, Jeff Krause. I showed him my pictures. I gave him a brief story of what was going on with me and he was very, very interested . He said he had to go and gave me his card with his phone number and his email and said to call him and we would get together at some time and I could tell him more of my story. He was very excited about it. Well I called and called and text him and text him and text him without any response. I did this for several months hoping to get back in touch with him to help get my story out. I told him I had a case file with MUFON and that the number was 81501 and that he should look at it and he would find it interesting also. Well after trying to contact him all this time one time and probably three or four months later, he finally text me back and said "don't call me, don't text me that I was delusional, I was making things up, I was lying about things and that I had made these pictures somehow and they were fake. I texted him back and said "please don't call me names and talk to me like that and I have not talked to you like that and have been very professional." Then I told him that the way he's treating me, he should not even be in the position he's in. I could not believe the way he treated me after being so interested and so intense when he was looking at the pictures and talking to me like this was going to be a sure thing. but it turned out it was not. I don't know what happened or why he changed his tune so quickly without even talking to me or hearing me out in any way and not checking my pictures out anymore.

I told Valerie Benco about this and she could not believe it and she told me I should get in touch with Chase Kloetzke who was a few steps below Jan Harzan the director of MUFON and that I should tell her what had happened with Jeff Krause to see if there was any other recourse to get my story heard and my case looked at. So I called Chase Kloetzke and got a hold of her secretary. I told her about the incident with Jeff Krause and she said well that was very wrong of him and that she would get me in touch with Chase. Chase did call me back and I told her what happened and agreed how unprofessional he was in saying what he did and that they were to take every case very seriously and that she was so interested in my case after looking at it. She said this is the story we've been waiting for. This is the evidence we've been waiting for. This pretty much shows us that they're real. She would continue looking into this herself and told me that I should get in touch with the leading investigator out of 5000 investigators, Robert Spearing. I got a hold of Robert Spearing and gave him a little bit of my case then told him that Chase wants him to look at the pictures that are in the case file; he told me he would rather see the originals and look at them.

For the first time ever I sent these pictures to Robert Spearing, who lives in New Jersey and would tell me if I had a case or not and if I could continue on with MUFON. I had never let them out of my sight and my bedroom is as far as they've ever gone. After his observation, he sent them back and said that his assessment was inconclusive, that I really needed to get a fingerprint expert to look at them. I tried to find a fingerprint expert online; there are only two of them and I tried to contact them by texting and calling them but I didn't get a response.

So I have my tickets to the next 2018 convention; my first in 2016 and they did not have one in 2017. The 2018 convention which was held in Pasadena and I had my tickets checked in my Motel room then went to the convention and showed the same people and even more vendors, more professionals and more of the cast of the Ancient Aliens Show. I continue to tell them that first contact is going to be February 2nd of 2022 and they all remembered me from the convention before I tried to get my word out. I stood up and told my story in front of the crowd as I waited for my turn in line in one of the big convention centers and told them that these pictures were of alien content they had a finger and a fingerprint of an Alien Being that were touched when they're developing and that we were going to have first contact February 2nd of 22. They looked at me and said, "okay do you have anything else to say?" But I just could not figure out why they were blowing me off.

During this time and after the convention which was probably three to four months after I tried to get a hold of the only two fingerprint experts that I found online that one day. I'm asking, yes I am asking the Aliens in my mind please help one of those fingerprint experts look at my story and my quandary and that I need to speak to them. Have them look at my pictures please and just help me get one of them to call me, text me back or contact me somehow.

I was just about to give up when the very next day I got a phone call from Robert May, one of two fingerprint experts who explained he runs a forensic laboratory that does all kinds of forensic work and expressed his apologies he missed my text and phone calls. He went on to say he would like to hear what I have to say and what I have to show him.

Now at first he didn't sound very interested because he said "I don't look at pictures; that's not what I do. I look at the fingerprint and decide on whose they are and try to find what crime they committed". He then said this was out of his wheelhouse. I asked him if he would at least be interested in looking at them to give me his opinion. He said sure that he would look at them, but he wasn't sure what I wanted to hear from him. He didn't think he had anything he could look at and check out to give me his opinion.

Well, I inquired about his fee which he replied was a $1,500.00 retainer and that would pay for 6 hours of work. His fee for each hour after was $250.00. I told him that's an awful lot of money; I could never pay that but,thank you for responding to me" and thanked him for his patience and his listening. Some time later, I was talking to my buddy TJ, telling him I was saving to hire Bob May. when he offered the money to me. Now TJ is my best friend from highschool and has been living in Las Vegas for the past several years. I hired Bob and for the second time ever, sent my original pictures to him in Michigan.

So in the interim of all this and my trying to get back with MUFON to see if they had looked at my case or if it had been passed up the ladder by any other investigators, directors or any of the Executive's that could help get this story out. In the meantime, I also went to all the news stations in town; Channel Ten, Channel Thirteen, Channel Forty and Channel Three. I took them each a set of my pictures, gave them my name and phone number; but in the two or three Stations i went to, I didn't even get beyond the receptionist or secretaries and, they said they don't do that and they would never do a story like this and was asked to please leave. I tried to leave the packet with them and think two of them gave them back to me, three of them just said it's time for me to leave; one of them I believe was channel 10, they said that they would give the packet information to John Bartell, the guy who would look into something like this subject. I got his phone number and gave him a little time to look at them. When I called and got a hold of him, he said he would take a look at the pictures and my story and get back with me. Well that never happened. I never heard another word from him and he would not answer my phone calls or return my texts. I would try to contact him a month later or maybe again two or three months later. I even tried again for two or three months and always nothing.

So by then the last convention came up in 2019 and by now, I had joined MUFON and was getting their hard copy monthly magazines, but never seeing anything about my story or my pictures in there. I purchased the VIP packet which cost me $300.00 for two years and never got anything out of it. As for the second year, I wasn't even going to renew my subscription but then I saw a bill for $300.00 on my credit card statement and found out they had just renewed me on their own. I was concerned so I called and spoke with Chase Kloetzke's Secretary who explained that I had not checked either box regarding the renewal and whether I wanted it again or not. They assumed I did, took my money and renewed the subscription for the next year. I told her that I was not going to renew because of what Jeff Krause did, the things he said to me and the way he treated me, so she said she could give me my money back. Then I decided to just keep it, but the year after that, only renewed for $99.00 only for their hard copy Magazine Subscription. Have to say though, it was even hard to renew for this because I was getting absolutely nowhere with MUFON; Chase kloetzke was not returning my calls or texts any longer.

I went to the next convention at the Los Angeles convention center in downtown LA and this time my wife came with me to stay with her best friend in Ontario while I went to the three days at the convention. We stayed at her friend's house for the two nights and I went to the convention each day, like always walking around showing my pictures and talking to the cast of Ancient Aliens talking to the producers again. They said they weren't ready for my show yet but they would be in touch with me. It was a great time to be there; this time I saw Eric Von Daniken, had my picture taken with him and told him that we are going to have first contact in 2022. He said he was ready and that he couldn't wait for it to happen and like everybody else had said, keep in touch at the next Alien Con with what I've seen and what's been going on with me.

I also saw Skeeter again, the Medium and had another session with her this time I taped it on my phone and boy was it interesting. I asked all kinds of questions like how old were the Aliens, were they millions of years or were they billions of years old? The entity called EGZYT who was channeling through Skeeter and said they were billions of years old. Then I asked if they were billions of years old and how they became a being. Did the first alien being rise from the pool of primordial ooze or was there a God that made the first being billions and billions of years ago? The answer I received was that it was a spark.

Now I was raised Catholic and I had to go to church and I went to all the classes necessary. I did all the different functions and I believe in God; it wasn't that I didn't believe in God when I asked the question. I was just wondering if God was billions and billions of years old and the answer that I received was that it was a spark that started life.

It had to be some type of Being like a God and not like the God's that we have been taught about in history; they were coming down from Heaven, descending to Earth, giving us fire and teaching us things. Those were the Aliens most likely from other planets that had reached the

point of evolution like we have. Perhaps they were given the same type of old technology like old spaceships and had drones like the Alien Grays that we've encountered on this planet. Of course they're not the original Aliens; these Grays were sent out on a mission to crash their vehicles on different planets that have evolved to our extent, then that technology was reverse-engineered on other planets and gave other Beings that have evolved the technology to gain advances in their civilizations and get them to the point of first contact.

When Bob received my pictures and was looking through them he was so interested that he told me he didn't want any more money. He was so enamored by these two pictures that he said "oh my gosh Buster, if these are what they are then we are going to be famous". He continued and said he had to do some more investigation on the pictures and it was probably another month before we talked again. By then, he looked at them through a microscope and he saw skin pores just like the ones we have that release the oils in our skin. These were made very similar to ours and that the ridge line structure of the prints were formed and the same height as ours. So as he kept checking the Polaroids he had more questions himself. He actually showed the photos to nine other experts in their perspective fields. One of them was a retired CIA Photography Expert that had been in the field for thirty to forty years, now retired but sure he would have been the one to talk to about old Polaroids and see if they could be faked. He told Bob you cannot fake those types of prints or photoshop them in any way. And the CIA photography expert also said that they were the most interesting things he had ever seen in his years of experience with the CIA.

ROBERT MAY

LATENT PRINT EXAMINER

Mr. May is a latent print examiner with over nearly 15 years of experience in forensic science. He is currently employed full time with a large state government forensic laboratory as the laboratory director, and was previously a latent examiner for the same organization. Mr. May is a member of the International Association for Identification (IAI), the Midwest Association of Forensic Scientists (MAFS), and the American Society of Crime Lab Directors (ASCLD). He maintains continuing education and advancement in his fields of expertise, regularly participating in professional meetings, workshops, and seminars.

Thomas P. Riley, B.S., *, **
Forensic Document Examiner
Michigan

Gerald M. LaPorte, M.S.F.S., **, ***
Forensic Chemist & Document Specialist
Virginia

Jeffrey Nye, M.S.
Forensic Biology & DNA Analyst
Michigan

Eric M. Cervenak, B.Sc.
Trace Evidence & Footwear/Tire Impressions
Michigan

P.O. Box 70, Frankenmuth, Michigan 48734-0070
Telephone (517) 394-1512 Fax (517) 803-4403

"A Global Footprint in Forensic Science"

Todd W. Welch, B.A., *, **
Forensic Document Examiner
Michigan

Jennifer Naso, M.S.F.S.*
Forensic Document Examiner
New York

Robert May, B.S.
Latent Print Examiner
Michigan

Marie Durina, B.B.A., GCAS*, **
Forensic Document Examiner
New York

Mr. Craig Johnstone
9200 Madison Ave #254
Orangevale, CA 95662

RE: Expert Report of Robert May, Latent Print Examiner

Riley Welch LaPorte & Associates Forensic Laboratories
Case No. 18-161621

I. I submit this expert report on behalf of Mr. Craig Johnstone. I have been retained by Mr. Johnstone to conduct a forensic examination and expert analysis of latent print photographs described in Section IV of this report.

II. I am being compensated $250 per hour in this matter and my compensation is not contingent on my findings or any testimony rendered.

III. QUALIFICATIONS

1. I am a latent print examiner with Riley Welch LaPorte & Associates Forensic Laboratories. I am also employed full time as the director of the Michigan State Police Forensic Laboratory in Sterling Heights, Michigan. I have permission to operate as an independent consultant in civil matters and have done so since 2008. My findings and conclusions in this matter do not represent the views of the Michigan State Police.

2. I have over 18 years of experience in the field of forensic science as a latent print examiner and crime scene investigator, all with the Michigan State Police. My training includes both latent print analysis and comparison and the processing of physical evidence for latent prints. I am also a certified operator of the NEC Automated Fingerprint Identification (AFIS) and FBI Next-Generation Identification (NGI) systems.

3. I am a member of several professional organizations, including the International Association for Identification (IAI), Midwest Association of Forensic Scientists (MAFS), and the American Society of Crime Lab Directors (ASCLD).

4. I have been an instructor in latent prints, digital photography, and general crime scene investigation for numerous evidence technician schools, having instructed personnel from the Michigan State Police, Detroit Police Department, and numerous county and local law enforcement agencies.

5. I have testified over 30 times in state district and circuit courts in the State of Michigan. I have never been excluded as an expert in any court proceeding.

**Diplomate of the American Board of Forensic Document Examiners, Inc.*
***American Society of Questioned Document Examiners*
****Fellow of the American Academy of Forensic Sciences*

www.rileywelch.com

IV. EVIDENCE RECEIVED FOR EXAMINATION

6. (Received via USPS Priority Mail from Todd Welch, tracking no. 9505510976078341265588, on 12/10/18)

   Item 1: Three (3) Polaroid-type instant photographic prints.

V. REQUEST

7. Examine photographs for evidence of latent prints.

VI. BASIS OF EXAMINATION

8. Friction ridge skin is a specialized type of skin found on the palms of the hands and the soles of the feet, including the fingers and toes. Unlike skin found elsewhere on the body, friction ridge skin consists of a series of ridges and furrows arranged in distinctive patterns. Individual ridges may deviate from a linear path (bifurcate), end abruptly (ridge ending), or display other unique characteristics referred to as minutiae. The relationship of these minutiae to each other is unique to each fingerprint, and is what enables a latent print examiner to identify a particular print left on a surface to an individual.

9. The fundamental concepts of latent print comparison and identification are those of uniqueness (no two fingerprints have ever been found to be identical) and permanence (barring permanent injury, fingerprint patterns remain the same throughout a person's life). Fingerprints begin to develop around the tenth week of gestation and, once development is completed, their patterns remain unchanged until death.

10. Latent fingerprints can be deposited though a variety of means such as sweat, skin oils, contaminants, blood, paint, impressions in soft materials, etc. There are a variety of methods for developing these prints to make them visible to the naked eye, such as powders, chemicals, or cyanoacrylate (superglue) fuming. In the case of porous materials such as paper, application of chemicals that react with the trace amino acids present in sweat are frequently used. Latent fingerprints developed on a surface may then be compared with known exemplars (typically captured with ink on a fingerprint card or, in some cases, using specialized scanners dedicated to this task) to determine if an individual made the latent impression in question.

11. When comparing the known and unknown print, a latent print examiner may reach one of three conclusions: (1) the latent print was positively identified to the individual; (2) the individual was excluded (meaning they could not have made the latent print in question); or (3) the results were inconclusive. An inconclusive determination results when either the latent or known impression (or both) lack sufficient quality to permit further comparison. The procedure is the same for known-to-known comparison.

VII. EVIDENCE ANALYSIS RESULTS

12. The submitted photographs were visually examined for latent prints.

    Two of the photographs support images of fingerlike impressions, including structures that reminiscent of human friction ridges. However, the morphology of these ridges is unlike that which is typically found in human friction ridge structure.

    - The images appear relatively clear, with minimal distortion. Edges are well-defined, with good contrast (nearly white ridges on a black background).

- Ridge flow is distinctly branched, with multiple bifurcations occurring within individual ridge paths. A "primary" branch runs nearly the length of the digit. most ridges originate from this primary branch. This contrasts with typical friction ridge skin, which is composed of discrete ridges that may bear deviations (bifurcations, islands, ridge endings and other minutiae) along their path.
- None of the common fingerprint pattern types (arches, loops, whorls) were observed.
- There are small voids along the ridges roughly analogous to pores found in human friction ridges. While ridges vary in thickness and edge contour, discrete ridge units are not readily apparent.
- Areas along the digit appear thicker, with individual ridges either minimal or entirely absent in the image.

VIII. CONCLUSIONS

13. The source of the fingerlike impressions was not determined. Neither the overall appearance nor individual ridge details conform to any friction ridge structure observed in the examiner's experience.

    It should be noted that while other animal species (gorillas, chimpanzees, and koalas being notable examples) are known to possess friction ridge skin, the basic appearance of fingerprints in those species is analogous to human fingerprints due to the similarities in morphological structure.

    If biological in origin, based on the examiner's training and experience it is highly unlikely that the impressions were made by human friction ridge skin.

IX. RETURN OF EVIDENCE

14. The evidence was returned via FedEx on 1/20/2020.

Robert J. May
Latent Print Examiner
1/20/2020

Fig. 1: Front of Photo #1

Fig. 2: Back of Photo #1

Fig. 3: Front of Photo #2

Fig. 4: Back of Photo #2

Fig. 5: Front of Photo #3

Fig. 6: Back of Photo #3

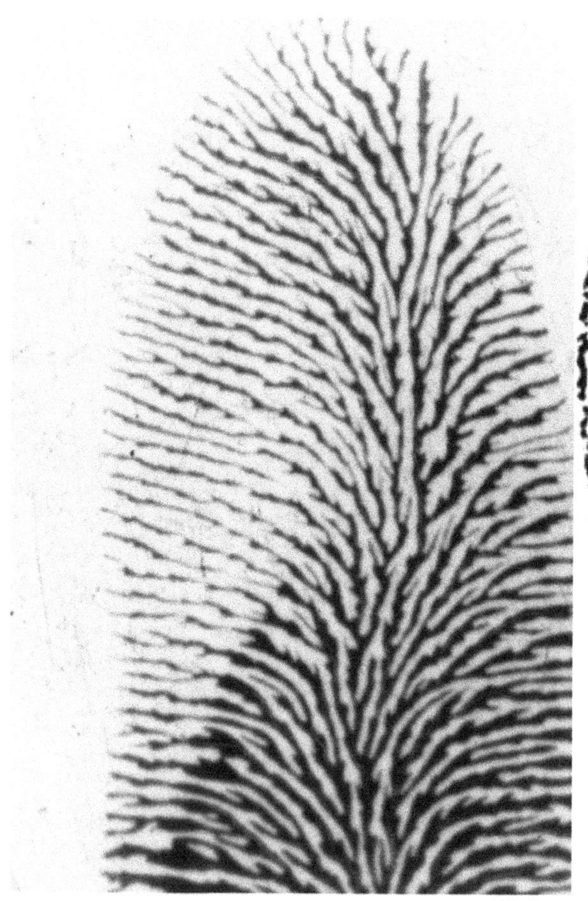

Fig. 7: Tip of unknown latent impression from Photo #2.

(grayscale; inverted for comparison purposes)

Typical known finger impression (double-loop whorl pattern).

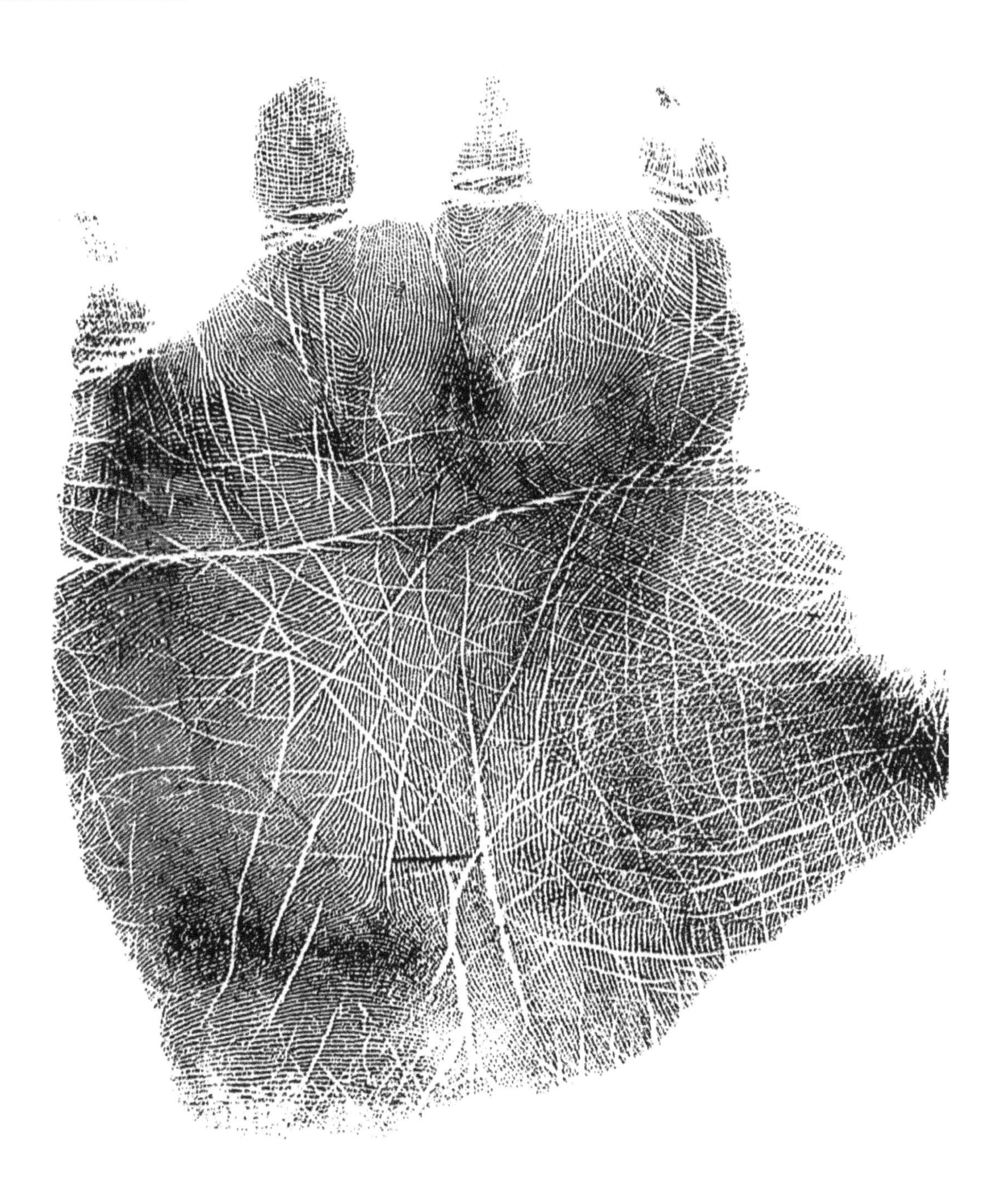

Fig. 8: Example of known palm print, showing typical friction ridge structure.

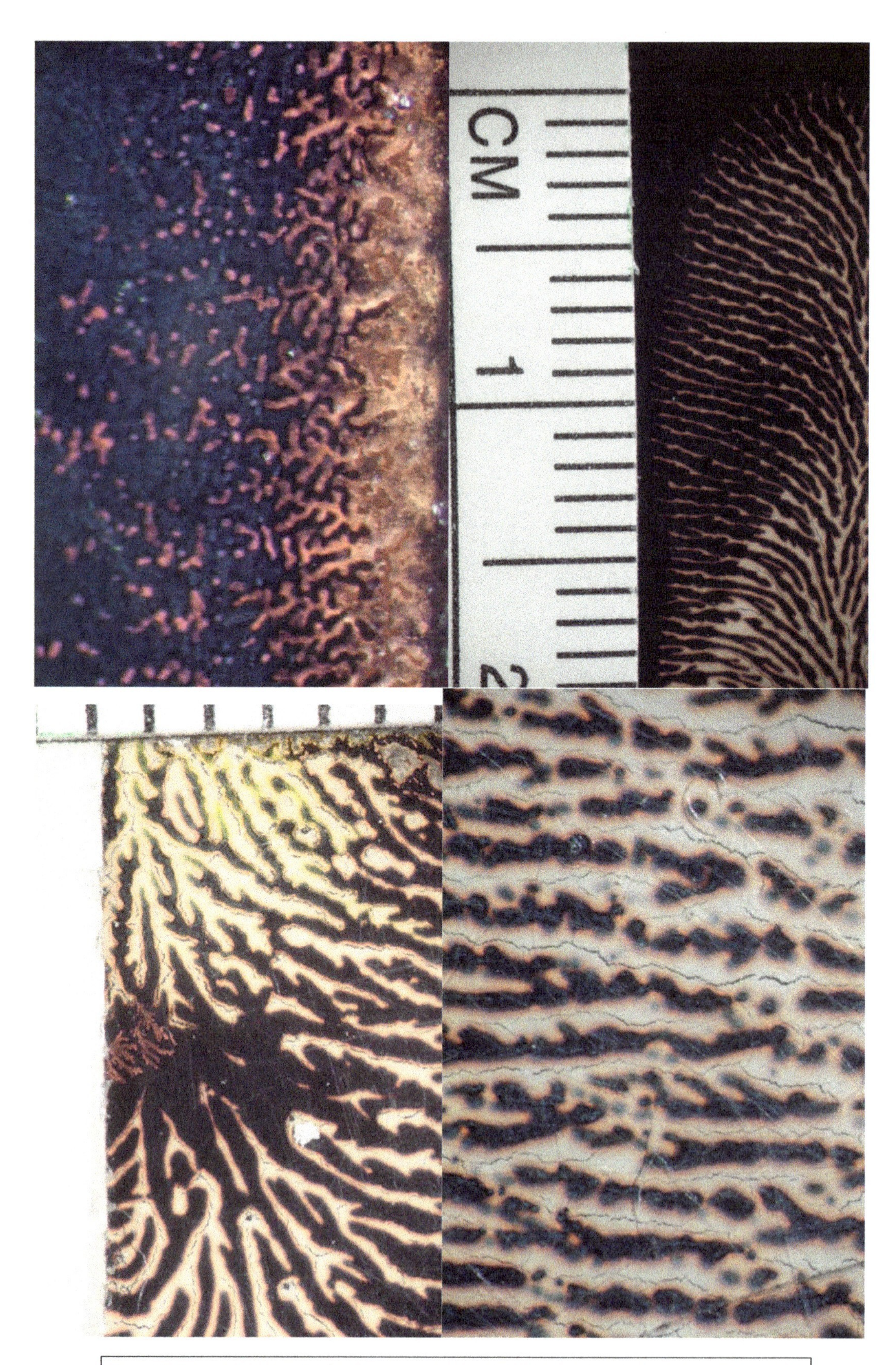

Fig. 9: Assorted detail of unknown latent prints (magnified).

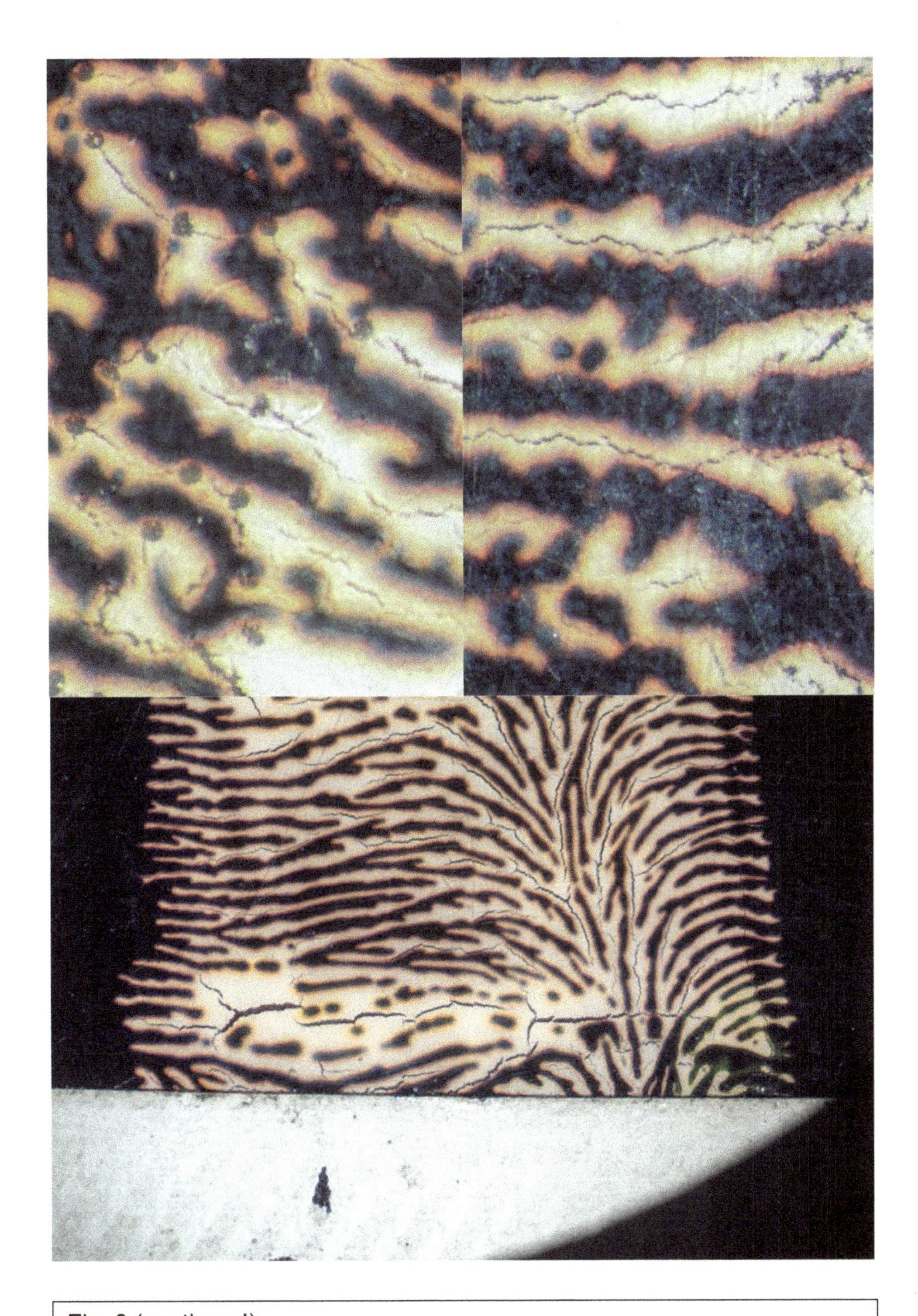

Fig. 9 (continued)

Fig. 10: Section of latent print from Photo #2. Note three-dimensional appearance due to ridge structure apparent in multiple layers of film substrate (white ridges on the right appear to be in a deeper layer than those at left).

Fig. 11: Small (~1 mm) branching patterns.

So I passed my opinion on to Bob that the reason that the Polaroids were able to be touched while they were developing and knowing that I touched every one of those Polaroids while they were developing before I set them in my house that it would have had to have taken a intense heat source to transfer an image at that point of development.

The heat source that I'm talking about is radiation. They would have been getting intense radiation from being in space and I think that was the way they were able to transfer their fingerprint onto the Polaroid. I passed that on to Bob and he said he would try to find an expert to check that out now; however, I really don't know if he found one and or if one of the nine other experts that he did meet with was a radiation expert. He wasn't able to put that in the notes of the official report I received from him nor was he able to put in any of the experts' names or their fields of expertise. He did say he was happy with the answers he received from the other experts regarding his questions he had about the Polaroids.

And on the side just talking to me as if we were sitting down at a bar having a beer is the way he put it he said these are the most amazing things he'd ever seen in his life and they sure do look like what you're saying they look like and with the report saying that the ridge structures of the fingerprints and the lines in the finger that they're-built in the same way humans are he called them ridge structures they are totally a different design but they rebuilt the same way as ours. The skin poor he saw deep inside the ridge structure of a human fingerprint we're reminiscent of a human skin poor that releases the oils in our hands.

He had to wait quite a long time in between each expert and the expert's time to be able to get together with him, but it was all worth it. Obviously each of the other experts were very knowledgeable in their fields or he would not have asked them to answer his questions. So I waited many months in between talking to Bob. It took eleven more months after that first month for Bob to finish the report which means he went to great lengths to get all of his questions answered.

I figured that after getting this report and getting it to my MUFON investigator, she would be so excited to get to this report and add it to my existing file. Well my investigator was going through a lot of family stuff and personal health issues that it took her probably three months to get the file with her report and the fingerprint expert's report to the MUFON Director, Jan harzan. But when Jan harzon did get the report finally he said this is very interesting and I really need to speak with the fingerprint expert that is the author of this report. So I got a hold of Bob and asked him if he would be able to talk to Jan harzan about the report. He was very interested in talking to Jan and said that he was moving from Michigan to Texas for a new job, but when he got situated he would love to talk to Jan harzan. So I waited for a while to contact Bob, probably a month and when I did get a hold of Bob he said that yes now would be the time and that it would be okay for Jan to get a hold of him. Jan finally did get a hold of Bob; however, Bob had some other stuff to take care of and as soon as he was done with that he would talk to Jan. Well just then the COVID-19 outbreak happened and Bob had issues at his work that he needed to take care of which led to not being able to talk to Jan until all those issues resolved with the COVID-19 outbreak were taken care of. Come to find out Bob and his wife both had the COVID-19 Virus which was quite bad and he was down for at least two months. His wife had it very minimally, but they were both doing good now.

Bob is ready to talk to Jan. When I was about to give Bob the okay to contact Jan, my field investigator Valerie Benko called me and told me not to let that conversation happen between the two of them. I was kind of befuddled as to why she did not want those to talk because he was the guy that was going to get my story going so the world knows we are going to have first contact. Turns out Jan got into trouble and now I would have to wait till a new director gets up to speed with his job. Then Valerie Benko would get a hold of the new director and fill him in on my story and tell him about the Polaroids and Bob's report.

Talking about things I've seen, one night while I was in my backyard as usual I was looking around and it was pretty late. I was standing in the middle of the basketball court, a concrete half court that I poured and was looking around when all the sudden I didn't hear anything but I saw something right over me. It was kind of rounded on the edge and it moved at a very slow pace; it was probably 2,000 feet above me. It drifted over me very, very slowly and as it drifted across the sky, I started seeing all the stars disappear. I mean as far as I could see, this thing covered the whole sky. I don't know if it was one or two miles wide but it was huge and it took quite some time for it to pass by. I could see that it was absolutely enormous like and I said it was dark but I could see the image because it was blacking out the Stars. It drifted very slowly, no noise as it came up over the hill and I just could not believe what I had just seen. I mean this thing was huge! I had told this girl that would move in with me later on. Before she moved in, she was living in Folsom, but I told her the story and she said she was outside that same night and saw the same thing. She wasn't going to tell me because she didn't think anybody would believe her but we both saw the same thing late that one night. Judy, this girl I'm talking about is now my wife for the last 16 years.

Each time I went to the Alien Cons I pretty much saw all the cast of the Ancient Alien Show, Giorgio Tsoukalos, David childress, Linda Moulton Howe who I had the 15 minute conversation with. Nick Pope, Travis Walton, and a couple of others. I would tell them each that we are going to have first contact in February of 2022 and would show them the pictures again and they would remember me from the last time.

So now I'm waiting for the next alien convention and I've started my book because there will be no more Alien Conventions for quite some time because of COVID-19. There was supposed to be a symposium in Las Vegas at the end of September 2020 I was really counting on. All the big military guys, all the big scientists and all the big government officials and anybody in an executive position in all those three categories, They were supposed to give their point and their views on Aliens and I'm sure a lot of them were going to say that Aliens are real,they're here we're getting ready for their first visit so everybody can meet them. When I gave my pictures to the fingerprint expert, Robert May, he showed them to an FBI expert, a CIA expert and a Homeland Security expert, top experts in their field. Now since they've seen those pictures and heard a little of my story from Bob and where he got them, I'm sure that now the FBI executives, the CIA executives and Homeland Security executives have all heard about my pictures and they even probably took some copies of them and sent them up the ladder.

Since then I have heard nothing but disclosure comments coming from the Pentagon, the Government Newspapers and the New York Times even printed that the Pentagon is saying now that Aliens are real. Some form of higher intelligence is controlling the UFOs or Unidentified Aerial Phenomena. The Pentagon is stating they are being intelligently controlled vehicles or manned vehicles that we are seeing up in the sky or in space that you can see with the naked eye.

One time I went out because a friend of mine called me and said I should see what's going on up in the sky, I went outside and looked up and I could see these little dots one right after the other with a huge amount of space in between just going across the sky. I would see one and then another, then another and another. This happened for a half an hour or better and across from the little lights that were coming across the sky I saw a flash across from them that would stay lit and then slowly go out, but it was directly across from the light that was continuing on. I have seen lights like this for many years.

When I was young and I was at the house alone for those ten years, I could go out on my patio and look straight up with the pair of binoculars I would lay down and look straight up through the binoculars and there was a white dot above my head every single day in the same spot I would lay there and look up and there it was every single day. There were days I would not look for a week or two but when I did go out with my binoculars and look straight up, it was there all the time, a light way up there. I couldn't see it with a naked eye, but with my binoculars could see this light would be in the same exact spot.

Just like the light when I took the pictures thirty years ago and the light that I saw up camping when I asked if I was supposed to be bringing the pictures out and going to the first alien convention.

So the symposium that was supposed to be at the end of September with all the executives is now rescheduled in July 2021. I am really waiting patiently to get there and to be able to show my pictures to them and to tell them all that I'm in contact with the aliens and that they gave me these pictures for the reason of being able to tell people that I'm in contact with them. Now the last I heard from my Bob he wanted to be at the symposium with me. I sent him the new date and time in July and the place where it's going to be held. As mentioned earlier in the story, he had since moved to Texas. I talked to him one time since his move there but since then, I haven't been able to get a hold of him. I have called and I have sent messages. I can only keep trying because he was so interested that he continued his work for me free of charge the next eleven months.

I can't wait for the next symposium in July of 21 hoping the whole cast of Ancient Aliens will be there and the producers of the show. I just saw the end of one of the last aired Ancient Alien Shows that Kevin Burns, the main producer passed away.

So I don't feel that I've ever been abducted or abused by the Ancient Ancestors but I do know for a fact that I've been taken and used by them for probably some physical type work. I would wake up in the morning and have bruises and I'd have three or four inches long gouges . There's times I would wake up in the morning and my tailbone would be so sore, like I fell really hard on something and it hurt for up to three weeks later. I would wake up and my wrist on my right hand was so sore I could barely even move it for probably four or five weeks. It hurts so bad and I had no idea how I could have hurt myself overnight. My bed is maybe two feet off the ground and I would have known if I fell out of bed and hurt myself that bad and I know that would have awakened me. There are countless times I have woke up with bruises on my arms and legs and my back to where my wife would see them and wondered what in the heck happened to me overnight.

I'm thinking the atmosphere where they take me is different than here on Earth because I must have had some type of mouthpiece. I have one solid Groove from both of my front upper teeth from one Edge up in a circular motion to the other side of my teeth to the other side and is a perfect half sphere. I have asked my dentist and the oral surgeon I went to how it could have happened that I have such a perfect circular groove in my two top front teeth. The answers they gave me was that my bottom teeth reached up and wore grooves as I was grinding my teeth while I slept. The problem with that is, my lower teeth aren't anywhere near long enough to go up that far into my top teeth and no way they could not have made a perfectly half circular groove in my two teeth above. Not to mention, my bottom teeth would have been ground in such a way that you would see the same wear pattern on my bottom teeth. Another funny thing is my top and bottom teeth have a gap and have never come together. Sometimes I wake up with bruises on my lower lips on the outside perfectly symmetrical on each side. This happens frequently and it's kind of unusual as it would dissipate through the day and by the next day you wouldn't see the bruises so they were not that bad; just noticeable when I got up in the morning. Another answer that I got from the oral surgeon was that I regurgitate my food and the acid that came up would eat away at my front teeth. None of my other teeth would be affected and the regurgitation fluids would create a perfect half-circle from one side of a tooth up and around over to the other side of; just The Two Front Teeth. For these reasons I know I have been abducted, but then again, I guess it's not an abduction when you want to go. I am waiting for my ride but I want to be coherent when that happens. I know at one point, I'll get one.

I'm not sure how else to get this word out about our first contact. I have tried a lot of different avenues. I hope this book brings light to a lot of different people, and the word will start getting out there that we will have our first contact February 2022. Less than a year away now and being blocked in many different ways for many years of getting this done. I know this has been happening to me for many, many years. I've had these gouges and bruises and aches and pains since I can remember when I get up out of bed and notice them right away.

Doing concrete for the twenty-two years that I did, my hips and my back would pop out as anyone who has done concrete work will understand. Well I would live with this for quite some time, in pain. It would get to the point where I would ask my girlfriend then, now my wife Judy to rub my back. She would get on this one spot where I felt it the most and asked her to rub as hard as she could. I had lived with that for years and would still go to work the next day, not taking any time to go to a chiropractor so it bothered me all the time. I would get home from work and it would start up because during the day, I'd be working so hard I didn't even think about it and I tried not to let it bother me. And then I did go to a chiropractor one time and he had to get up on the table and climb up on my back and push as hard as he could with all his weight to try to pop my hips and back in place it took two or three visits but he finally got it put back in place. It would work for a while but then I would do something that would pop out again and wasn't actually sure how it was happening. I was 185 pounds for ten years of solid muscle, so I'm sure that when I popped out and the reason it took so much for him to get my back and hips in place was because of all the muscle surrounding that joint. I would go on for a while like that and then remember thinking I wish I could get this thing to pop in without having to go to a chiropractor three or four times a week and spending all that money just to get it popped in one time. So this had been going on for quite a while, over a year and it was pretty painful. After I got off work and went home, I would sit around watching TV and then go to bed. It was even hard to go to bed. Well I was out on the job one day and I was walking backwards picking up stakes, cleaning up a big concrete job and as I would pick these stakes up, I would throw them in the bobcat bucket my cousin was driving in front of me. There was a lot so he was helping which was kind of unusual; he never really helped me, but he knew I was out of joint. Still walking backwards cleaning up the job site, I got too close to a slight drop off in the customer's property. This was a spot where a hose had been running water for quite a while and when I moved it, I went to throw another stake in the bucket and slipped in the slick spot on the hill. It really jarred my hips; I mean it hurt like crazy that I had to stop for a while. Probably a good half an hour I took just to relax but then went out with the wheelbarrow and just picked up the rest of the steaks myself instead of the Bobcat. My back was really hurting on the side where the joint always popped out my right hip side. Later that day I went home and on my way home, stopped and got out of the truck. When I got back in I had kind of realized that my back wasn't out of joint anymore and that the pain I felt as I slipped on that hill was my hip popping back in place. Every now and then it would pop out a joint.

We were in Oklahoma at my wife's son·s house and he, his friend and I went out to play some frisbee golf. Well I'm not real good at it but I guess he and his friend were, so I was watching them play for a little bit. I decided I would play and then retrieved my frisbee, went up to the line to throw it and my first throw, I popped my hip out of the joint really bad. It was so bad that I had trouble walking. So I went back to watching them play the rest of the game and walked around with them even in pain. We had a couple beers on the way home and when we got there, we tried to find a chiropractor we could contact Sunday morning. It was later in the day Saturday that I popped it out of joint. Sunday, we called and called and called chiropractors but there are no chiropractors open on Sunday even for an emergency visit. The last phone call we made, somebody actually picked up the phone and we told him my problem as well as visiting from California. He said he was just there picking up some paperwork but to go ahead and come on in. I thought what a cool guy so we went down there and when I walked in he had me get up on the table and lay down. He felt exactly right where I told him it was separated. He knew exactly right what I was talking about. Well he had to also get up on the table and put all his weight into trying to pop it back in. He tried and tried but to no avail. He told me to go ahead and come on in the next day and that he would give it a try again and told him that sounds good, but it kind of felt like he popped it in a tiny bit but not very much. It was just enough to take the hard pain away. On our way home my stepson's and was talking to his buddies how they wanted to play some beer pong so we stopped and bought some beer. Well when we stopped he got an eighteen pack of Bud light bottles and I got a twelve pack of Heineken bottles and then drove home. He had a lot of stuff to bring in so I grabbed the beer, one in each of my hands and walked slowly up to his house. It was dark and I couldn't see hardly anything but I knew there was a tree coming up in front of me. I walked around the tree but I didn't see the tree root coming up out of the ground. I kicked that root so hard with my right foot and while carrying the bottled beer in each hand, it caused an instant pain in my back; it hurt like crazy on my right side. After walking into the house, I walked over and set the beer down and continued to walk around a little more and noticed that trip fixed my back. Just like the last time when I slipped on the hill it was still a little sore, but wow! It was back into its place. So we played that night and probably drank too much. The next day I called the chiropractor and told him what happened and how my back got fixed;

he said that was very unusual but good and he was happy for me. That's two times that it was just out of weird circumstance that my back got fixed. Now I'm not saying that the Aliens helped me in that respect but it was very unusual for my back to get put in the way that happened.

I quit doing concrete in 2007 when the crash hit and I lost my job as a concrete laborer. By then I was no longer working for my cousin's business, but instead for a concrete company that made pools. We did the concrete around the pools such as walkways, patios and such. Well when I lost that job I tried to find another job in another line of work. I didn't want to go back into concrete which was seventeen years at that point. All the applications that I put in I couldn't find a job for nothing. Nobody would get back to me with every application that I put in. I never heard back from anybody. I was pretty concerned because my wife was working and I hadn't been working for quite a while.

So while I was off work all that time, the muscles in my upper body which were probably about forty pounds, started diminishing because I wasn't doing any work. As the muscles dissipated my joints started loosening up, my neck started popping, my shoulders started popping, my hip started popping and as I lost more muscle mass my shoulders would pop out a joint. My hips would pop out of joint and my wife could hear my neck pop while I'm out in the living room and she's in the very back bedroom . It was so loud that when she came out of the room she would ask me if it was my neck she heard popping. She would be next to me hearing it pop at times and knew how loud it was. So that went on for quite some time, probably three or four years and I had many problems with my hips and shoulders popping out of joint. It was pretty bad but I was to the place where I didn't need a chiropractor anymore; I could pop it in myself, especially my shoulder. I could grab my arm between my knees and pull back on my shoulder and that would usually put my shoulder back in place. My back wasn't so easy and I called the chiropractor for many years and got to the point he would bring a table over to my apartment and adjust me right at home. I think it was $60.00 each visit he came over but that was better than having to go to his office. Then he retired but I was so thankful he still continued to come over to my place and pop me back in.

It was probably four or five years this was going on and then one day I had a little wooden step stool out because I was putting some things up and I was cleaning the little knick-knack shelf hanging on the wall above the couch. As I was cleaning this knick knack shelf and moved to standing on the cushion of the couch. I was standing there cleaning and when I was done, started to step down off the couch cushion, but had forgotten that I had not put the little step stool away. When I stepped back off the couch backwards, I stepped down with one foot and stepped back with the other foot onto the step stool that I didn't remember was there and I fell straight back. I fell flat on my back, hit my head and the whole back of my body slammed the floor. It was pretty bad. I hit really hard. After I got up and started to check myself and see what I had done, I started to walk around a little bit to see if I was okay. When I started walking around I felt my hip was back in place and my shoulder that I was having problems with was back in place. As I went through that day I finally noticed that my neck wouldn't pop like it was popping.

I went a couple weeks walking around just to see if little things would pop my hip out and if my shoulder could get popped out by doing things I did before and it didn't pop out of place. I began getting up in the morning not having to pop my neck or just very slightly. Then a month went by and I hadn't popped my hip out, I hadn't popped my shoulder out and my neck wouldn't pop like it used to so that fall on the floor and falling backwards stepping down from the couch backwards and that step stool being there somehow fixed me. Now I don't know what are the chances that could ever happen again, but since that day which has probably been a good ten years now, my hip doesn't pop out of place, my shoulder doesn't pop out of place and my neck only pops a little bit now. That fall fixed my hip and my shoulder and my neck all at once.

Now that I'm pretty sure it was set up by whoever is watching over me and who has watched over me all my life. Like the times when I was younger, I have had incidents happen where I have been so close that I should be dead. One time we went camping up to Rollins Lake or Wright's Lake somewhere up in the Crystal basin there was a gigantic Rock sticking out of the water probably thirty feet tall so we took a raft out to that rock, my sister brother and the Stewart boys. We got up on the top of that rock and I watched the Stewart boys and my brother jump off that rock all day long; it had been a couple hours since I watched them jump. They would do this thing called a Belly Dive because you could see the rocks down below. The big rock and some giant rocks down there and you had to just miss them by diving out and doing a belly dive well. I finally got up the nerve and they prodded and pushed me enough to where I got up there and decided I'm going to jump off this rock and I'm going to do this belly dive the same way they had done it all day long.

I got my courage up and I ran and jumped and I dove out as far as I could but still wasn't sure about this belly dive thing and as I dove in my head grazed one of the giant rocks down below. This one was probably three feet underwater. I grazed my head just enough to make a scratch that I had blood on my forehead; another quarter of an inch, maybe an eighth of an inch I would have split my head wide open. That was one of the closest times that I knew someone was watching over me and that I had help there.

Another time was when I had my mustang and it was a very fast car. I was jamming down Madison Avenue coming up to Hazel Avenue and I probably had smoked a little weed at that time, and I hit the gas going across Hazel Avenue not aware that a red light had just came on over my head and the traffic was coming the other way. Just as I went through the intersection I saw a car coming to the back side of me and I knew that car barely missed me. Then as I looked forward all in a blink of a second the car in front of me passed right in front of my car and had to have just missed it by less than an inch. I know that those cars missed me but were so close; it was like I wasn't even there yet I knew I was there and saw it happen just out of my peripheral both ways. That had to have been alien intervention also and not my time.

My uncle had come from Minnesota and we were doing concrete work in the truck my dad had before he passed away. My uncle knew I was a mechanic so he brought the truck over to my house and we were working on it. I would be the one to replace the Universal Joint on the driveline and my cousin was up in the engine bay working on taking the spark plugs out and my uncle was in front of it doing the oil change. I was getting all the tools together to begin to take out the driveline.as they jacked up the truck. My driveway was on a slope and being a professional mechanic, I should have checked to see if they blocked the back wheels, but I didn't. So my cousin was up in the engine bay, my uncle up in front doing the oil change. While the front wheels were up off the ground, I was taking the driveline out and as I loosened the last bolt to take it out and the pressure of the whole truck was on the driveline. Because the brakes weren't locked and the wheels weren't blocked the pressure forced the driveline down right towards my head; it came like a bullet. I was able to move fast enough for it to hit the concrete instead of my head but I knew that truck was coming down and I was going to get crushed as it's rolling down the hill. I'm trying to scoot sideways to get out from under the truck well as I'm trying to scoot my one shoulder would come up and then my other would shoulder would come up and as my left shoulder came up the transmission crossmember grabbed my shoulder and as I was a little sideways it rolled me up on my side and I knew at that second I needed to pump my whole upper body up as hard as I could. As I tightened my muscles, the truck crossmember pulled my shoulder up and the whole weight of the front of the truck was on my left arm and at that second that I was vertical and heard this pop. My cousin up under the hood had jumped down and was trying to hold the truck from rolling backwards because he knew I was underneath it. My uncle was in the front trying to hold the bumper. As they were sliding down the driveway along with the truck, my cousin said that he heard an oak tree break. Well the sound of oak tree breaking was actually my left Humerus snapping from the weight of the truck on me. Now the Tranny crossmember was probably 8 inches off the ground normally, but from one side to the other side, my shoulders were probably eighteen to twenty inches across so the truck raised that whole foot extra with all the weight on my shoulder. When my arm snapped and it rolled me over, just at that time I tried to move my leg in; I saw the right tire was heading for my left leg. The tire actually rolled over my leg but it didn't hurt it at all. I didn't feel a thing as the truck rolled down into the street and as I was laying there looking up after I turned back over, looked over to my left and I could see my arm was a foot away from my body. Well that's how it looked like or is what my mind registered. I don't know how that happens, but it looked like my arm was a foot from my shoulder. It turned out my Humerus separated and snapped in half and that's just how it looked.

My cousin jumped down and asked if I was okay. When I told him I think I broke my arm and it's sitting over there. That's when he told me it was right up next to me, then he went into the house phone in the kitchen and called 911. There I am laying in my driveway answering his questions as he's yelling at me for my address. Meanwhile the nurse was asking if the person who was hurt was answering all these questions and he told her yes, the guy that got run over by the truck.. Help arrived and I went to the hospital and got fixed up. They didn't put a cast on it, they put a plastic shield over it and wrapped it up and said they were going to let gravity pull my arm down back into place. Well that kind of didn't work as how the bone healed is right up towards the skin and my muscle is in a different spot. The way it healed, I can feel the bone right below my skin. Now when I was under that truck and it started to pull me sideways, I heard this voice in my head saying pump up and that's what I did. I pumped up as hard as I could. And it was such a split second that I just did what it said and I know that voice came from whoever was helping me.

Another time my now ex father-in-law from my first wife asked me if I would come up and help him cut wood at friend Red's land up in the hills. I told him I would since I would be off that Sunday. So we drove up to this guy's property, his wife and my ex wife went along. I went out cutting wood and we were out there for a long while when we came to this one three-tiered oak tree it had three big trees coming out of this one main trunk. We fell three trees and one of them had a big Branch pointing down into the dirt. Well it was pretty much stuck there so I got on the other side of the tree and rolled it up a little bit so he could start cutting this big looped branch off. As he was cutting this branch, he was getting closer and closer to me with that chainsaw. He was probably sixty-five to seventy years old at that time and he's getting closer to me. I started yelling at him, he's getting awful close but with the chainsaw running he couldn't hear me and he kept getting closer and closer. Trying to get out of the way, I reached over and grabbed hold of the other side of the tree real tight with my left hand and then with my right arm, lifted it up off the branch he was cutting because he was really close. As I lifted my arm off of that branch, he raised the chainsaw and the top side of the chainsaw hit the bottom side of my arm while it was running. When he stopped the chainsaw and I looked at my arm and I only said whoa boy! I pulled my arm back but didn't look just then; I thought he had just grazed me but when I pulled my arm forward I looked, there was a half inch gap to the bone in my arm and I just went 'oh my God!' I probably said a few cuss words I'm sure, now thinking that I'm going to be out of work for who knows how long. I'm looking at my arm dripping with blood and a half inch gap to the bone. My little finger and my ring finger on my right hand both dropped and I could not move them. He grabbed a handkerchief out of his pocket and just wrapped it as tight as he could to keep the blood from pouring out. Then he took his jacket off and wrapped it up then we started driving to the cabin where his friend, his wife and daughter were and when we got there, they called the

Roseville Hospital and they called the surgeon on call. We drove to Roseville and it was another time that I could have easily lost my hand. It was probably two inches down my arm from my wrist and it took many hours for him to stitch me back up. Now that could have also been way worse, and I'm thinking that I probably had help getting my arm out of the way; or the rest of the way so I didn't lose the whole thing.

When I went back to the doctor for my follow ups, every time he would thank me so many times for getting the movement and strength back in my hand, but it was my only right hand so I did everything I could to help myself get it back in shape. I would thank him when I went in and he would thank me five or six times before I left, because I would do my exercises and hand squeezers all the time to get my strength back and my movement. I don't have any feeling between my ring finger and my little finger, but have full use of my arm and hand today. People actually commented on my strength to this day. And no one would ever want to wrist wrestle with me.

So back to the mind bending vision that I go into and dark outside, would find a place without any light pollution so I could concentrate and I can look and see these energy swirls all around me. What I'm thinking is these energy swirls are an alien presence in the next dimension. Now when I see these energy swirls I can concentrate on the middle of them and see them travel around. When I start following these energy swirls as they're moving around, I may lose them every now and when I do, a little light flashes right in the middle of the swirl, like it's directing me back to it. I'm following them around and will see another one flash in its center and like it's trying to get me to watch it also. Sometimes there may be three or four of these energy swirls and if I concentrate hard enough I can actually keep two, maybe three of them in my vision until they try to separate or move around and that's when I lose them. It's very hard to keep each one in my vision and. I take it as part of my training. I can see these things anytime and mainly when it's not so bright out or lights inside are slightly dim. These swirls will try to get my attention at all times of the day or night. I have these flashes and I try to follow these swirls when it happens. I feel it's good practice to continue learning more and more about what this whole other world is about. Now I'm really not sure what is next in the learning phase before we meet our Ancient Ancestors February 2nd 2022 to be exact.

What we have seen that archaeologists have dug up here lately is really proving that there have been many civilizations through many millions of years on this Earth. They just found a hammer and the head of the hammer is 99 .9% Iron, and the hammer handle is petrified. Now to petrify a piece of wood takes one to two million years depending on the conditions to actually absorb the minerals from the dirt and whatever ground it is in at the time. They just found an iron pot with two little pour tips at each end and this iron pot was found in a 300 million year old coal seam. Now it takes a long long time for coal to form and a lot of pressure and I mean a lot of pressure that pushes down on land mass over millions of years to create the pressure to create coal. This is not an easy process or a fast process and for this iron pot with two pour spouts at each end like a gravy bowl was definitely made by man and to have ended up in this coal seam for millions of years old. 300 million years is what they dated this coal seam back to.

Archaeologists also found an ancient wagon wheel buried 300 feet underground. This was a wooden wheel and it was in the ceiling of the shaft they were digging and the wood that it was made out of was petrified. Now how could someone explain how else that wheel got where it was, how this gravy bowl got where it was and how the hammer that was found where it was other than the civilization that made them were millions and millions of years old.

And I feel that the civilization that we live in today, we have come to the point where we have learned and taken the knowledge that the aliens have given to us in their old technology in flying saucers that have crashed on Earth. I'm sure that a two mile wide spaceship that they have now would not be able to be shot down or crash on Earth with the technology they have now. I'm sure those smaller spacecraft that have crashed and we have back engineered, we're actually given to us and the Gray Beings that were in them when they crashed were drones. I believe that Aliens can make new universes. They can take an empty part of space and have the ability to make big bangs. If we're making miniscule big bangs in the CERN collider, they can make big bangs now.

When these big bangs happen they let the planets form and the sun's form for a while - a couple billion years. And when it's time they seed the universes with DNA they let it go to drift around and land on formed planets, in the primordial ooze and when life evolves to the point we have as Human "Beings", we are knowledgeable and have good brain sizes. They visit the planets and just like us they gave us bigger brains, they gave us more intelligence, they gave us speech all in a process when we're now ready for it.

Once we've evolved to the point where we are very intelligent, they will crash their old technology vehicles here and help us learn about them and how advanced they are. We just came out of the horse and buggy era less than one hundred years ago. We have been to the Moon, we're going to Mars, we have the CERN Collider in less than one hundred years; we've come 5,000 years worth of technology in a short time when you think about it.. I don't think that just happens on our own; we were helped along, we were given that technology and we expanded on it. Now we have the ability to blow our planet up, we have hydrogen neutron atomic bombs and could destroy our planet. We have the ability to totally destroy ourselves but they have brought us up to this point so they don't want that if we are going to have first contact with them.

They have helped us along and shut down whole missile silos that house nuclear warheads. We have sent scientists and engineers to see what happened to these missiles; they have torn them apart to try to find out. And when they couldn't find out what actually happened to them, our engineers and scientists all put them back together and as they finished assembling them it's like the switch was turned back on and they were all ready to go again. They are millions if not billions of years older than we are so we are going to learn a lot more at first contact with them.

I think that we are going to have to leave this planet at some point and we're all going to need to have new blood that can handle this and I believe that I have the blood that is going to be distributed with my donation. And I'm sure that other people on this Earth have the same blood I do and are also donating and distributing to the masses and when we're ready, we're going to all load up on a spaceship and go to another planet. Maybe it's because our sun is too close to us and is going to blow up or something along those lines and when that happens we'll have to leave.

I have been getting these flashes for a very long time at different times and in different locations. I get them at very unusual times as sometimes I see them on a wall, sometimes in my car on the dash, sometimes as I'm driving see them over to the right in the trees. I have white flashes and I have black flashes. The white flashes seem to be good flashes because I see them when I'm thinking good thoughts. When I'm thinking about stories that I'm going to be telling in my book I'm getting them when I do things good and believe it's kind of praise for me. I get black ones with negative thoughts. I get black ones for not doing the right thing or not saying the right thing. I get black flashes when there's things that I shouldn't be doing. I'll get a black flash on an item like when I was drinking too much beer, I'd get up and I'd go to the refrigerator to grab another beer and I got a black flash right on that beer as I was reaching for it. I hadn't even grabbed the beer yet. I mean it was a very intense big black flash so I left the beer in the refrigerator and pretty much quit drinking beer at that point Every now and then I'll have a beer or two when son barbecues up at his house for Father's day, birthdays and stuff like that but very rarely do I have a beer anymore. I was drinking too much coffee quite often even though I knew it was bothering my stomach and shouldn't be drinking it but I did. I went to reach for that next cup of coffee this one time, a big black flash came on the coffee pot, I knew then I needed to stop drinking coffee so I did. Very rarely will I drink any coffee now. I put a little freeze dried Folgers in my hot chocolate at work but that's just for taste more than anything.

Now whenever I get a little worried I get a nice white flash. One time we went up camping and I was kind of wondering if they're around me now and flashes came around me bright as any.. I get flashes thinking about things that happened in the past and Aliens would have had to have had a hand in. I get flashes when I should be writing my book and not watching TV. Flashes happen outside when I'm looking up in the sky. As I said before there were hundreds of flashes that I saw, then the Jeep commercial and the flashes in the field when I went to drop my son off after I had him for the weekend. They are a good thing they keep me in check and I feel I use them wisely choosing my choices. I know things are going good when I see white flashes and change my direction when I see the black ones. Sometimes I see flashes so bright and big they're usually off to one side of my vision left or right. And now I'm seeing them more often because I haven't been real focused on getting my book done.. Every once in a while I see a little round circle; sometimes it's all day long but sometimes it's not for a week or two with a solid circle in the middle of it and it's very intense and visible and sometimes it's almost invisible. I see these round circles in my telescope way out in space as I'm looking at a supposed star. There is a round circle with a dot in the middle of it that's supposed to be a star, but I wasn't really sure what it was.

There are times it appears in my vision like when I'm driving down the road I will see this black dot in my vision or if I'm standing out of my balcony it'll show up and I'll try to follow it keeping it in my vision. With the black in the middle of this circle and as I'm watching it, try to move it across my vision; sometimes it just stays in one spot and I can't get it to move or it will move all the way across my vision the other way. When I go back to try to pick it up and try to move it to the other side, it'll jump real fast to the other side. It's kind of like it's questioning my thoughts and moving ahead of what I'm thinking; pretty cool stuff. I've seen this little round circle for years, probably more than twenty or thirty years it's pretty strange that sometimes there are two of these in my vision and there have even been up to thirty, maybe forty of these little round dots in my vision following from one side to the other and it kind of freaked me out when I saw that many at once that I kind of just snapped out of it and they all went away.

Well I thought it may have to do something with the shots that I get in my right eye. I get shots in my right eye because as you get older the veins in your eyes get weaker and about a year ago one of them burst in the middle of my eye and created this little Cloud. This all started when I went to my eyeglass doctor and he said that I probably had something a lot worse going on than what he could fix so he referred me to an eye specialist.

I went to the eye specialist and they have a special optical camera which can take very detailed pictures inside of your eye and saw a blood vessel had popped. It was a cloud of blood that I was actually seeing in my vision so they would give me a shot in my eyeball and I could even see the fluid coming through my eyeball as he was injecting it; pretty weird. I usually get an injection every four to six weeks and by the next day the cloud usually dissipates at a rapid pace but then all the sudden, I saw all these little round dots flying all around in my vision and it kind of worried me so just kind of kept blinking until they were gone and they haven't really came back until I started asking to see more unusual things.

So here lately I've been seeing more dots in my vision and it's only at certain times they just kind of capture my vision and I follow them for a little bit and then they go away so they seem intelligently controlled and like sometimes they just mess with me. I've gone back to asking to see more and more special things in my vision. I would be standing in the bathroom going pee and I would kind of go into this vision just a slight bit. The slight bit that I go into this I see little squiggly lines, little flashes and I can see the little swirls with the flashes right in the center of them. These little swirls I see are the energy swirls of aliens trying to get my attention and as I'm watching these things move around and trying to keep my attention I have been seeing what looks like little brakes in the Time Dimension; like I am actually seeing into another dimension as this little break happens. It looks like a crack opens up and they're bluish white for right now because they're very minimal and I haven't seen a whole bunch of them. but I'm starting to see more of them.

As I see more of them the duration of the time that the care is actually open has been increasing so sometimes I see whitish-blue sometimes I see a little darker color in it and it's like I am actually seeing something on the other side of our dimension. I'm saying they live in the next dimension and I think they can create new Dimensions which are new realities on a different frequency by making big bang's in empty space and creating whole new Dimensions with galaxies and universes all across space and time, but needs new Dimensions and different frequencies. So I believe when I took those pictures, they stepped out of their Dimension into our Dimension into my living room my photos and stepped back either that or being down from that spaceship that I've been taking pictures of.

On top of the flashes in my eyes I have like invisible worms in my eyes can be very long and when I'm not in a real great mood or I'm down or depressed or something bad just happened these worms are almost invisible but I can see the edges of their lines. And the lines are all curled up in a ball and when I'm happy and everything is going good or something fun has happened they straighten out. Sometimes when I kind of wonder about something, these worms form little designs like when I'm wondering about something it'll form like a question mark. Sometimes they have a form of a face that's sometimes pretty weird. I see these worms pretty much all the time in my vision. Sometimes they're very pronounced, sometimes they're faint, sometimes they are much larger or much smaller. At times they are very thin but long and at times they are very fat and I can't see the whole worm.

I have refrained from telling my eye doctor seeing that I would probably be in a straight jacket by now. But I have been asked by my specialist now and my previous eye doctor if I see flashes, but the flashes I see are very specific when they happen; they don't just happen all the time. It happens when I'm thinking something positive or thinking something negative and they're either a white flash or black flash, so I know I do not have random flashes in my vision. These are very specific and then when I'm looking out into the sky into the clouds I can see these little tiny flashes or sometimes they're even very pronounced flashes. Like wow they are very intense. Sometimes the whole part of the sky that I'm looking at, I see flashes or little squiggly lines shooting off. I try to follow these flashes in the sky and they can sometimes take me around in a full circle as I keep track, This one flash that's actually like a dark spot in the sky and as I'm watching it move across the sky and if I lose it a little bit I'll see the flash in the middle of it and connect right back up with it.

Animals and I seem to click. I had a Maine Coon cat when I was young name Titters and he probably weighed twenty-five pounds. He slept with me and would come outside with me; he was an outside cat and one day he turned up missing. I was pretty upset about it so I tried to look for him but couldn't find him anywhere, then years later I was working at a 76 Gas Station at Madison and Hazel and talking to one of the mechanics there about my cat missing years ago. That's the subject we were on so I just mentioned it and he said that he remembered a cat just like that showing up at the gas station. So he had crossed Madison and Hazel Avenue to get to that gas station. I hoped he found a good home and lived for a long time after. The point I'm making is that I get along with animals really well, dogs in particular. I've been able to walk up to dogs where the owners have said that the dog doesn't like men and I would ask if I can try to pet them and they say no problem, go ahead and that dog would just sit there and let me pet him and rub him for as long as I wanted. And this happened most always to the point where my wife calls me the dog whisperer. Dogs just walk right up to me and just like today, a Great Dane walking with his family where we were walking out on the trails in back of our home; and this Great Dane stood up over half my length and walked right up to me. He wasn't on a lease but he walked right up to me, stood right in front of me and looked right up at my face. I reached down and started rubbing him and scrubbing his neck and he loved it. My wife told the people well you better come get your dog because he's going to be stuck there for a while if my husband has anything to do about it. But just right then the dog looked at the people walking off and he went and joined them. Walking on these trails out there are dogs that want to come to me and the owners would have to yank on their leashes to try to get them to come back to them. All they want to do is come over to me; it's some attraction that they have to me. I guess they can sense good people.

During the years that I was being shown all these alien type things getting me ready for first contact and being able to tell people that it is going to be okay to meet them. I had a cat named Misha. I got this cat when I was married to Sharon in 1986. I had Misha for twenty almost twenty-one years before she passed; that was a devastating event for me. My connection with the cats I've had has been very personal. Like when Misha couldn't hear for the last three years of her life, I would come walking in the door after work and just start thinking about her and she would come out and be right by me and she always slept with me. I lived with her for a many years and we went through a lot together. She was a very important piece of my life. She had an alien face on her back that I've taken pictures of when I got myPolaroid Camera and I took several pictures of her to show the alien face on her back as part of the proof of my alien contacts. Misha was a Calico Siamese Mix and weighed about 8 lb. Now we have Rosco and he is a Maine Coon and Russian Blue Mix. My wife Judy heard about two kittens that were put out of a car on the side of the road and a Good Samaritan picked them up and took them to a kitten shelter. This shelter was in Davis and my wife called and asked if they were still there and sure enough they were and she asked me if she could go pick up one of the kittens. Just before Rosco, we had our cat Peach who we had for about seven years. She was my sister's cat and when she had to move she had to get rid of her. She was a little shy so we had to work with her and she finally came around. She had kidney issues and we tried everything from a special wet food, trying to add water in her dry food and even gave her Saline IV's to try and keep her hydrated because she wasn't drinking enough. Finally we had to euthanize her when kidneys completely shut down. It had been a while since Peach passed away when my wife asked if we could get another kitten. That's when Rosco joined our family. Why I'm telling these stories about animals that I've had and the contact I've had with dogs is to do with my believing that these animals come into my life for a reason. Because of who I am and the alien connection that I have.

Rosco wanted to go outside when he was a kitten and he was always looking outside watching us leave out the door and trying to get out the door with us. He would go out on the balcony and watch all the other cats outside. We have feral cats around that live in the alleyway between the two Apartment Buildings behind us; one woman feeds them, one woman lets them come in and stay the night and she leaves her door cracked all day so the cats can go in and out. We bought a harness and a leash for him and put it on him and he laid right down. Well I took him down the stairs to let him know he could go outside with the leash and the harness on. When I set him down at the bottom of the stairs he laid down again, so I brought him back upstairs, took the harness and the leash off and told him we're going to do this my way. I grabbed a little camping stool, opened the door and told him we're going downstairs. I sat there on the sidewalk and I let him go from one end of the sidewalk to the other end and only where I could see him. I would tell him to stop when he got to the end of the sidewalk and if he didn't stop I brought him upstairs; he hated to be picked up and brought upstairs and still does. So we went out again the next day and did the same thing for about 3 months. We stayed on the front sidewalk and I did not let him go any further than that. He could not go out in the parking lot. It was only to the edge of the concrete curb that he could go. After about three months of training and his going where I told him we would go down the sidewalk a little further. I told him to stop and if he did not stop, I brought him back upstairs. We now walk around our entire Condominium Complex and he takes the sidewalk from one area to another, never going into the street or parking area.. We have a Greenbelt behind the entire complex which goes out to Nimbus Lake and he loves to wonder out there and explore too. Of course the lake is about two miles away and I'd never let him go that far, but he's been out there quite a ways sometimes.. My wife or I are always with him and he's never been unattended; we're no more than twenty to thirty away. He really minds just like a dog and our Community are amazed about how well behaved he is. Some of our neighbors even ask while we're out, "where's your dog" which is funny. He understands commands and minds them too. When he started to Chase squirrels or birds I'd let him go so far and then tell him to stop and if he kept going I would pick him up and bring him back in the house. We would go out the next day and we went out, I'd let him chase the birds or the squirrels for a little bit and tell him to stop and he listened and did what I told him to. He learned he doesn't like being picked up and carried home.

When Rosco was one year and three months old, we came in from our walk one evening and were preparing to give him his evening treats when we noticed his breathing labored and we knew that was not right and had to take him to an after hours animal hospital where he spent three days. They put him in an oxygen tent and got a hold of a cardiologist as it turned out to be his heart. It was quite bad and we were really concerned about him making it through the night. We were willing to do all we could for him, but did sign a DNR because we needed to consider his quality of life if it came to that. Fortunately, he did make it and the cardiologist came to see him the following day when we learned his diagnosis was Congestive Heart Failure, but the doctor thought he could be saved. He now goes in every eight or nine months for an annual check up on his heart. It's expensive, but he's worth it.

Rosco celebrated his fifth birthday in April 2021 and is a lien sixteen pounds and three and a half feet long. He takes four different medications and three of them twice per day. We're so blessed we can give the best life possible and he knows it. I feel he was sent to us by the aliens; he needed us and we needed him..

I went to fish aquariums and stood right at the glass and stared at some fish and one of them came right up to the window and stared right back at me. I tried standing in the same position or walked to the side as I kept my eyes on him and he followed me all the way across the aquarium. It was pretty strange but I see that I have a connection with animals and they have a connection with me.

Hummingbirds buzz me everywhere. I hear the chirping of them up in the trees all the time when we go on walks or anywhere I go. I'll be downtown Sacramento, in San Francisco or in the mountains and I hear them and they buzz all the time. The house I lived in on Rich Hill, there was a hummingbird and he was an old guy. He was around for many years. He came to my back door where I had a hummingbird feeder and I would see him all the time. He protected that hummingbird feeder and wouldn't let any other hummingbirds drink from it. That was his so pretty much he was my hummingbird. I knew it was a male, was dark green and he was pretty fluffy and he was big for a hummingbird . I would see him through the year for many years. One year there was a big storm that came through. I could see the trees out in the backyard flailing left to right and had to have been six to eight feet. They were moving so hard and fast the wind was blowing extremely hard. The following morning I woke up and I came to the back door and I looked up at the hummingbird feeder and the hummingbird came flying over and sat on the ledge of the hummingbird feeder and looked right at me; his beak had been broken and was pointing down towards the ground. I was just devastated and could not believe that happened to this poor guy. I didn't know what to do but knew I couldn't really do anything. I couldn't catch him and what would a vet do anyway; I just had to let nature take its course. I saw him fly back over to his tree so I walked through the backyard and looked up into the tree in my backyard and there he was sitting there. He looked at me and I looked at him. I was so sad, pretty sure I cried when I walked back into the house. I could look through the peephole at the front door and at a certain time of the day or night the light would catch the front stoop just right and I could see a hummingbird etched into the concrete similar to the one in Peru as one of the Nazca lines.

Having a great relationship with animals of all kinds, and their sense about a Human Being, I also have a good sense that Alien Beings have brought us up to this point; they have given us their old technology and if they didn't want us here, we wouldn't be here. I believe their visit is going to be a great thing.

My take on the whole thing is that the Aliens have been around for a very long time. I'm talking about millions of years and they ruined their bodies in that they can't reproduce because of the radiation that they deal with in space travel. That's why they've used our women to procreate and keep their race going. Are Ancient Aliens benevolent and it will not be a bad thing when they show up and show themselves to the whole world and not just our Government or our Military and that is why disclosure is happening right now. We are all going to need to know that this is happening so the War of the Worlds scenario does not happen.

We don't need to be shooting at them or trying to kill them. They are way more intelligent than us. They have been around for billions of years and they can travel Universes, they can travel through Dimensions. I'm even sure they can travel through time both forward and backward. They have been around us and manipulating our Wars and bringing us to the point of first contact and think prior civilizations have either gone awry or did something wrong as a whole community and we're wiped off the Earth. Other civilizations that have proved themselves and are good enough to be contacted have been.

We are about to have our first contact in our lifetime. This is happening to us and I have had my own contact with them and I have told many about it. This is something that they have done over and over throughout our Galaxy, other Galaxies with other planets that have evolved to our point a revolution.

So since my pictures have been circulating with the FBI, CIA and Homeland Security and other Entities of our Government for the last year the Pentagon has now requested all of those Entities begin gathering all material about Aliens and Alien Crafts that they have and get it to the Pentagon within six months so that the Pentagon can begin disclosing to the public. so they can know that aliens are real. They have been around and helped us and they brought us up to this point of evolution and we are ready whether the Military or Government thinks we are as a society or not. I think that the covid-19 virus that is going on right now and for the past year has to do with weeding out the weak, unhealthy or people not fit to go on a lengthy trip, which it is doing around the world.

I have seen the faces of many different types of Aliens and one of them is an owl face so we should all get ready to meet people or Beings from other planets in different solar systems and accept them as our brothers and sisters. We will be inferior to their knowledge and discoveries. We will learn so much from our Ancient Ancestors and other Beings from other planets and that this is a great time in our future and a Turning Point for Humanity.

Lightning Source UK Ltd.
Milton Keynes UK
UKHW051923140621
385498UK00006B/232